Unity 2D Game Development Cookbook

Over 50 hands-on recipes that leverage the features of Unity to help you create 2D games and game prototypes

Claudio Scolastici

PUBLISHING

BIRMINGHAM - MUMBAI

Unity 2D Game Development Cookbook

Copyright © 2015 Packt Publishing

First published: February 2015

Production reference: 1120215

Published by Packt Publishing Ltd.
Livery Place
35 Livery Street
Birmingham B3 2PB, UK.

ISBN 978-1-78355-359-4

www.packtpub.com

Credits

Author

Claudio Scolastici

Reviewers

Marcieb Balisacan

Si Fleming (PhD)

Marcin Kamiński

Pranav Paharia (Game Nick: Fi.eol)

Robin Petersson

Commissioning Editor

Akram Hussain

Acquisition Editor

Subho Gupta

Content Development Editor

Sumeet Sawant

Technical Editor

Utkarsha S. Kadam

Copy Editors

Gladson Monteiro

Merilyn Pereira

Vikrant Phadke

Project Coordinator

Danuta Jones

Proofreaders

Simran Bhogal

Stephen Copestake

Maria Gould

Ameesha Green

Paul Hindle

Indexer

Tejal Soni

Production Coordinator

Shantanu N. Zagade

Cover Work

Shantanu N. Zagade

About the Author

Claudio Scolastici is an Italian game designer with a background as a researcher in the fields of psychology, artificial intelligence, and cognitive science.

He is employed by Italian game developer SpinVector as Technical Game Designer and Unity specialist.

In November 2013, he released a book titled *Mobile Game Design Essentials* for Packt Publishing, as well as tutorials about AI modeling and scripting at Digital-Tutors.

To those who never told me to look elsewhere...

About the Reviewers

Marcieb Balisacan is an independent game developer, designer, and producer working in the Philippines. With a background in computer science and multimedia, and more than twelve years experience in development in the games industry, he has been releasing games for various platforms and mobile devices. He has been previously invited as a technical reviewer in publications from Packt Publishing covering game design and development topics using CryEngine and Unity. He has cofounded a game development studio startup, Full Mana Studios, and is the Lead Game Engineer at Synergy88 Studios, in which he is leading the design and development of computer games.

> Marcieb would like to acknowledge his newborn son, Aedan Chord, who kept him awake during the review of this book and inspired him to move forward.

Si Fleming (PhD) is a senior engineer in the games industry with a career spanning over a decade. He holds a PhD in computer science from the University of Sussex where his research focused on distributed systems, ad hoc social networks, q&a, security, and privacy. Dr. Fleming has taken part in game jams, including #OneGameAMonth, and is currently working on several indie game projects.

Marcin Kamiński is working for Artifex Mundi as a senior programmer and also owns his company Digital Hussars. Previously, he has worked for CI Games and Vivid Games. His main fields of expertise are artificial intelligence and network programming. For 14 years, he helped develop great games for PC, consoles, and mobiles.

Marcin was also the reviewer of *Unity iOS Essentials, Packt Publishing*.

Pranav Paharia is a game designer and developer with more than 2 years of experience and expertise in technologies such as Unity3D and Cocos2d-x. He has experience working with numerous game technologies such as RPG Maker, XNA Game Studio, Construct 2, and more. He is proficient and passionate about gameplay and graphics programming. As well as coding games, he likes to spend time on his own prototypes.

His passion for gaming comes from being a hardcore gamer with a true e-sports spirit. He has spent over 6 years playing *Counter-Strike*, and has participated in many tournaments. He is very dedicated to gaming and feels it's the proudest part of his life.

He finished his Bachelor's degree in information technology from VIT University, Vellore, where he was inspired to work on game development technologies. Determined to carry on his passion and turn it into his profession, he then joined DSK Supinfocom International Campus where he opted for the video game programming course. He spent a year in various endeavours of designing and developing games before joining an indie game studio where he worked on award-winning *Song of Swords*—a 2D RPG game showcased in NASSCOM GDC 2013. He also worked on 3D mobile games such as *Chotta Bheem Laddoo Runner*, *Fish Gone Mad*, *You Are a CEO*, and more.

As well as games, he sometimes likes to work on other aspects of game development, such as designing game loops, user acquisition strategies, and monetization models, and content writing.

Being a game enthusiast, Pranav is always interested in new game technologies and how it brings excitement to the lives people. You can contact him at pranavpaharia@hotmail.com or visit his portfolio link: http://pranavpaharia.wix.com/portfolio.

Robin Petersson is a level designer from Sweden. Being a passionate gamer, he has focused on game development almost all his life. He started out as a Flash developer, learning ActionScript 3 and making small indie games for the Web. As a level designer, he uses both his artistic skills as well as his scripting knowledge to create unbelievable gaming experiences for players all around the world. If you are interested in Robin's work, please visit his portfolio at http://iamrobin.se/.

www.PacktPub.com

Support files, eBooks, discount offers, and more

For support files and downloads related to your book, please visit www.PacktPub.com.

Did you know that Packt offers eBook versions of every book published, with PDF and ePub files available? You can upgrade to the eBook version at www.PacktPub.com and as a print book customer, you are entitled to a discount on the eBook copy. Get in touch with us at service@packtpub.com for more details.

At www.PacktPub.com, you can also read a collection of free technical articles, sign up for a range of free newsletters and receive exclusive discounts and offers on Packt books and eBooks.

https://www2.packtpub.com/books/subscription/packtlib

Do you need instant solutions to your IT questions? PacktLib is Packt's online digital book library. Here, you can search, access, and read Packt's entire library of books.

Why subscribe?

- Fully searchable across every book published by Packt
- Copy and paste, print, and bookmark content
- On demand and accessible via a web browser

Free access for Packt account holders

If you have an account with Packt at www.PacktPub.com, you can use this to access PacktLib today and view 9 entirely free books. Simply use your login credentials for immediate access.

Table of Contents

Preface

There was a time when building games was a cumbersome and almost exclusive activity, as you needed to program your own game engine or pay a good amount of money to license one.

Thanks to Unity, creating video games today is still a cumbersome activity, though less exclusive and expensive!

With this book, we aim to provide you with a detailed guide to approach the development of an actual 2D game with Unity. As it is a complex process that requires several operations to be performed, we will do our best to support you at every step by providing all the relevant information to help you successfully make games with Unity.

Packt cookbooks offer knowledge in the form of recipes that describe individual tasks and how to perform them. This way, you are provided with a quick-reference guide that you can read in whichever order you may see fit for your actual development needs.

We thus encourage you to freely move back and forth between chapters to take full advantage of the flexible structure of cookbooks.

Enough of the premises, let's start by taking a look at the Unity interface!

The goal

In the last decade, a large section of the game development industry moved back to its garage roots, so to say, and opened its arms to embrace small groups of very motivated people who want to make games. The revolution of (almost) free 3D engines such as Unity and UDK allowed these small groups with no money to invest to give birth to their gameplay ideas and challenge the market by building up actual, professional games.

With this book, we plan to provide you with a detailed guide to approach game development with Unity. As game making is a complex process that requires several operations to be performed, we will do our best to support you in each step, providing all the relevant information to help you successfully move through the creation of your next game with Unity.

This book provides knowledge in the form of recipes that describe individual tasks and the steps required to perform them. This way, you are provided with a quick-reference guide that can be checked in any order you see fit for your actual development needs.

We thus encourage you, the readers, to freely move back and forth between chapters and take full advantage of the flexible structure of this book.

The mean

As a reference template to help you better understand the practical operations explained throughout this book, we plan to create a game prototype, featuring 2D gameplay with 3D graphics.

We believe this solution nicely fits two distinct needs: on one side, 2D gameplay is lighter to prototype, allowing us to describe the many features of Unity without the burdens of 3D mathematics.

On the other side, using 3D graphics (specifically for the game character and other game objects), we have the opportunity to discuss very important Appendix features of Unity, which would go unnoticed elsewhere. In the end, Unity is an engine to make 3D games, mainly!

The interface

With regard to the operations described and the pace we move between topics at, we assume you are already familiar with the Unity interface and its basic operations. Anyway, for those of you who may be a bit rusty with the Unity pipeline, let's begin our journey with a quick look at the Unity interface and the operations required to start a new project and configure the folders directory.

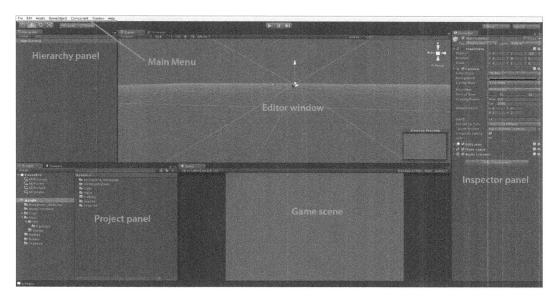

The preceding image shows the layout we are used to working with in Unity. Let's give a quick description of the main panels and windows available:

- **Main Menu**: This is where you **Load\Save** projects and game scenes, create and import new assets, and create game objects of different types to be added to the game scene. This is also the place where you add specific components to game objects to improve their features.

  Finally, this is where you configure the **Render** and **Project Settings** and where you configure the **Build Settings** for your games.

- **Hierarchy panel**: This panel lists all the objects that have been added to your game scene so far. Here you can select a specific element to be manipulated in the game scene or add components to improve its behavior and capabilities.

▶ **Project panel**: This window lists the project folders and their contents. If you want your Unity project to keep nice and clean, we suggest you make extensive use of folders, by adding one specifically for each type of game asset (models, animations, textures, audio clips, animator controllers, and so on) you plan to have in your game. This way, whenever you need to access a certain asset, you know exactly where to search for it!

The following image shows an example folder directory of a project of ours:

▶ **Editor window**: This is the main Unity panel, the one that is used to actually assemble the game. Any GameObject that is required by your game must at some point be instantiated (by physical drag and drop or by code) here!

▶ **Game scene**: This panel shows what the game looks like from the player's perspective. It displays the output of the main camera from the game scene and it is very useful to actually test what's happening, especially when you are studying specific graphic solutions or the disposition of GUI elements on the screen.

▶ **Inspector panel**: This panel allows you to edit the assets available in the **Project panel**. It contains a lot of functionality, and we will often refer to the **Inspector panel** and the object properties displayed here, especially upon importing new assets (**Models**, **Animations**, **Textures**, and **Audio clips**) in our project.

If this super-quick description doesn't suffice, we recommend you go online and check for a beginner's tutorial about Unity. There are plenty available, both for free and for a price (for example on www.digitaltutors.com). Unity itself offers plenty of resources; you could start with this one: http://unity3d.com/learn/tutorials/modules/beginner/editor.

The words

As mentioned, we assume you are familiar with this interface and know how to navigate between panels. We also assume that you have a clear understanding of the basic terminology of making games: you know what a mesh or a material is, you know what we mean when we talk about animation clips and timelines, you know what a collision or a particle system is and what GUI stands for...don't you?

The assistants

As Unity is not provided with an embedded editor to create graphic contents (both 2D and 3D) or audio, we look to third-party software to accomplish these tasks.

With regard to graphics, we assume Photoshop (CS6) as the reference software for 2D images and Maya (2014) as our 3D editor of choice. These are both worldwide industry standards, and we believe that by taking this decision, we are actually helping you get familiar with tools that, sooner or later, you will have to confront in game development.

Still, as this book focuses on Unity, we take care of providing you with the required graphic assets to follow the recipes, as we cannot afford to provide you with a guide to powerful software such as Photoshop, Maya, or Blender. We encourage you to learn at least the basic operations with these software, as it will help you better deal and take advantage of the power of the Unity engine.

Start a new project in Unity

We are now ready to start a new project and deal with the Unity project directory.

When starting a new project in Unity, we are asked to set a name for it and add what we need. Follow us in the next recipe, which shows you how to perform this fundamental task.

Getting ready

Assuming you have already installed Unity, you are nicely ready to proceed.

How to do it...

1. Launch Unity. The **Project Wizard** window opens to start a new project.
2. In the **NewProject** tab, select a destination directory and type a name for the project. Our choice is `Unity_Cookbook`.

3.   No need to flag any packages from the list. We will import packages as we need them through the development process. Simply hit **Create**. You can look at the following image for reference:

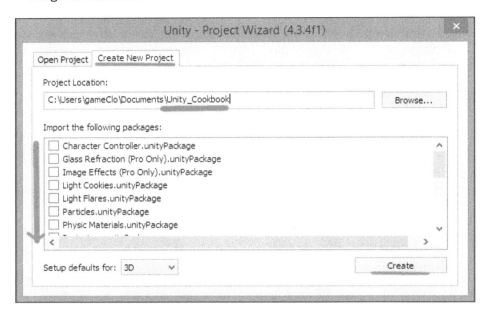

How it works...

Well, this is fairly simple. Unity sets a new project in the chosen destination directory, creating a file structure to store anything required to run the project, edit it, and upload additional contents to be used in the scene.

Adding a folder to the project directory

Getting ready

We just need a new open project to perform this task, so you should be ready from our last recipe.

The file structure

We are almost ready to begin working on our project. We would just like to have a look at the structure of the directory we are using for this project and explain the criteria to effectively manage it.

The following screenshot displays the structure of the directory with an example list of folders:

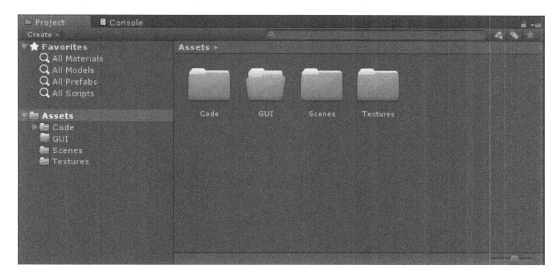

As you can see, we have a number of folders, one for every important asset that we are planning to use for the game. We prefer having all different types of assets well separated in a reasonable and meaningful number of folders, so we always know where to search for what.

For now, we just have one folder for the coding, one for the interface elements, one to save our game scenes, and the last one for 2D textures.

If you think we don't have enough folders, well, you are totally right. But don't worry, the list is going to grow very soon, starting with our next recipe!

With this next recipe, we'll show you how to add a folder to our project directory. Stick with us!

How to do it...

1. In the **Project** panel, right-click anywhere in the window and select **Create\Folder**, as shown in the following screenshot:

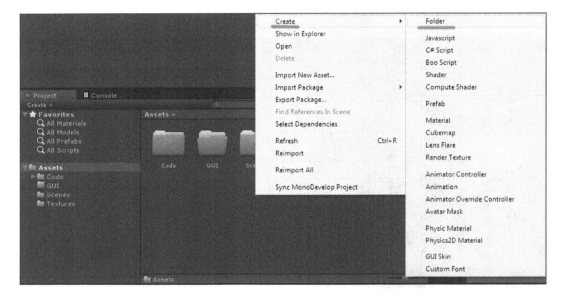

2. Type a name for this folder. We recommend the name **Models**, so we can use this folder to import **Models** by following the recipes of the next chapter:

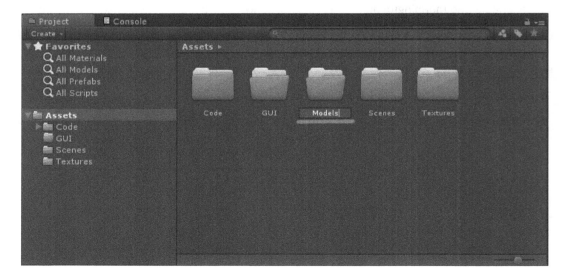

How it works...

Unity is extremely flexible with regard to adding\moving folders\files into its **Project** structure. Folders can be equally created inside or outside the software interface, and files can be both imported or simply copied from one folder to another outside of the software environment. When the focus gets back to Unity, it automatically updates changes we made. Thanks Unity, we appreciate that!

What this book covers

Making a game from scratch is no easy task. Games, even those that look basic at first glance, are a collection of elements, or assets, belonging to different fields of practice and requiring distinctive skills to be assembled.

With this book, we aim to provide you with what you need to know to make games with Unity.

Each chapter covers a single topic and provides a set of practical recipes to learn how things are actually done in Unity.

The following is the list of topics we cover with this cookbook:

Chapter 1, Importing 3D Models and Animations, deals with the process of exporting 3D models from Maya into Unity and the operations required to correctly set up imported FBX with models and animations in Unity Inspector.

Chapter 2, 2D Assets for Unity, explains how textures are imported in Unity, how to set them up, and what a texture atlas is. It also deals with materials and how to add lights to a scene.

Chapter 3, Animating a Game Character, discusses Mecanim, the built-in tool to animate characters in Unity, introduced with Unity 4. It explains how to import and configure animation clips, how to create transitions between them, and how to blend animations.

Chapter 4, Taking Control, shows how to improve the graphic appeal of your character by adding a normal map to its material, and it also introduces the topic of game controls, explaining the difference between the Character Controller and the Rigidbody components.

Chapter 5, Building Up the Game Level, shows how to create the assets to build up an actual game level made of platforms and gaps for the character to jump. We also implement the game controls and improve the gameplay by adding collectible game objects.

Chapter 6, Game Scenes and the Graphic Interface, explains how multiple scenes are added to a game. We also introduce the topic of finite state machines to control the screen flow of the game. Finally, we explain the basics to create a Graphic User Interface.

Chapter 7, Improving the Gaming Experience, shows you how to add audio to the prototype, by importing and configuring audio clips. We also introduce Particle Systems and show you how video clips can be played in the scene.

Chapter 8, Sprites, Spritesheets, and 2D Animation in Unity, deals with sprites, spritesheets, and sprite animation. It also explains the features of the built-in Sprite Editor of Unity.

What you need for this book

As Unity is not provided with an embedded editor to create graphics (both 2D and 3D), we look to third-party software to accomplish these tasks.

We assume Photoshop (CS6) as the reference software for 2D graphics and Maya (2014 edition) as our 3D editor of choice. These software have world-wide industry standards and we believe that by choosing these reference software, we are actually helping you get familiar with tools that, sooner or later, you will probably have to confront.

Still, as this book focuses on Unity and we cannot afford to also offer a guide to such powerful and feature-rich software, we took care of providing you with the required graphic assets required to better follow our recipes.

That said, we encourage you to learn at least the basic operations with Maya and Photoshop, as well as any other 2D and 3D software that are popular among artists and game developers, as this will help you to take advantage of the power of the Unity engine.

Who this book is for

This book is intended for professionals, game developers, and hobbyists who are interested in making games with Unity.

Sections

In this book, you will find several headings that appear frequently (Getting ready, How to do it..., How it works..., There's more..., and See also).

To give you clear instructions on how to complete a recipe, we use these sections as follows:

Getting ready

This section tells you what to expect in the recipe and describes how to set up any software or any preliminary settings required for the recipe.

How to do it...

This section contains the steps required to follow the recipe.

How it works...

This section usually consists of a detailed explanation of what happened in the previous section.

There's more...

This section consists of additional information about the recipe in order to make the reader more knowledgeable about the recipe.

See also

This section provides helpful links to other useful information for the recipe.

Conventions

In this book, you will find a number of text styles that distinguish between different kinds of information. Here are some examples of these styles and an explanation of their meaning.

Code words in text, database table names, folder names, filenames, file extensions, pathnames, dummy URLs, user input, and Twitter handles are shown as follows: "We can include other contexts through the use of the `include` directive."

A block of code is set as follows:

```
(public class PacktController : MonoBehaviour {):
public float horAcceleration;
  public float cruiseSpeed; //max speed when not pressing
  public float maxSpeed; //max speed while pressing
  public float actualSpeed; //speed at given time
  public float limY; //limit on y, use as mathf.abs
  public float expon; //used to smooth vert movement speed
  public float alpha; //use to tweak the vert movement
    speed
```

New terms and **important words** are shown in bold. Words that you see on the screen, for example, in menus or dialog boxes, appear in the text like this: The **Bumped Diffuse** shader requires two textures, as we stated before: the diffuse map for the **Base** color and **Normalmap** for the lighting details.

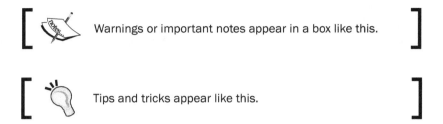

Warnings or important notes appear in a box like this.

Tips and tricks appear like this.

Reader feedback

Feedback from our readers is always welcome. Let us know what you think about this book—what you liked or disliked. Reader feedback is important for us as it helps us develop titles that you will really get the most out of.

To send us general feedback, simply e-mail `feedback@packtpub.com`, and mention the book's title in the subject of your message.

If there is a topic that you have expertise in and you are interested in either writing or contributing to a book, see our author guide at `www.packtpub.com/authors`.

Customer support

Now that you are the proud owner of a Packt book, we have a number of things to help you to get the most from your purchase.

Downloading the example code

You can download the example code files from your account at `http://www.packtpub.com` for all the Packt Publishing books you have purchased. If you purchased this book elsewhere, you can visit `http://www.packtpub.com/support` and register to have the files e-mailed directly to you.

Downloading the color images of this book

We also provide you with a PDF file that has color images of the screenshots/diagrams used in this book. The color images will help you better understand the changes in the output. You can download this file from: `https://www.packtpub.com/sites/default/files/downloads/3594OT.pdf`

Errata

Although we have taken every care to ensure the accuracy of our content, mistakes do happen. If you find a mistake in one of our books—maybe a mistake in the text or the code—we would be grateful if you could report this to us. By doing so, you can save other readers from frustration and help us improve subsequent versions of this book. If you find any errata, please report them by visiting `http://www.packtpub.com/submit-errata`, selecting your book, clicking on the **Errata Submission Form** link, and entering the details of your errata. Once your errata are verified, your submission will be accepted and the errata will be uploaded to our website or added to any list of existing errata under the Errata section of that title.

To view the previously submitted errata, go to `https://www.packtpub.com/books/content/support` and enter the name of the book in the search field. The required information will appear under the **Errata** section.

Piracy

Piracy of copyrighted material on the Internet is an ongoing problem across all media. At Packt, we take the protection of our copyright and licenses very seriously. If you come across any illegal copies of our works in any form on the Internet, please provide us with the location address or website name immediately so that we can pursue a remedy.

Please contact us at `copyright@packtpub.com` with a link to the suspected pirated material.

We appreciate your help in protecting our authors and our ability to bring you valuable content.

Questions

If you have a problem with any aspect of this book, you can contact us at `questions@packtpub.com`, and we will do our best to address the problem

1
Importing 3D Models and Animations

In this chapter, we prepare the assets to build up our game prototype, starting with the process of exporting 3D models from Maya, our 3D editor of choice, into Unity. We also take care of correctly setting up the imported models and animations in Unity Inspector once they get imported.

In this chapter, we will cover the following recipes:

- Setting up a scene in Maya
- Using groups to rotate FBX files
- Exporting FBX files from Maya
- Configuring imported FBX files in Unity
- Exporting animations
- Configuring imported animations in Unity Inspector

Introduction

When building up a game, we usually start by importing the graphics assets to actually build up and prototype the gameplay.

In this specific case, we decided to begin with 3D models. Before importing the models, you should take care of bringing in the textures. Feel free to switch between *Chapter 1* and *Chapter 2*, *2D Assets for Unity*, which focuses on textures and materials. A cookbook is specifically designed to leave the readers free to access the contents in whichever order they prefer.

We assume that you have the assets to test the operations explained throughout this book; in case you don't, you can download the contents available on Packt Publishing website.

When importing models from a 3D software into Unity, there are several settings to be defined: scales, source materials and textures, rigging and animations, and many others. We will discuss the most important setting soon.

For the importing process to be fully successful, it is also important that the scene in the 3D editor is properly set. When modeling stuff with a 3D editor for a 3D engine, it is important that scales, lights (if available), and cameras match between the scenes, or your models won't fit the game levels properly.

For the recipes of this chapter, we decided to pick Maya as our reference 3D editor. We do not mean that Maya is the best software, but there are plenty of reasons for this choice. Native Maya files are supported by Unity, and the LT version of Maya allows you to perform "one-click-exporting" of Maya scenes directly into Unity (`http://videos.autodesk.com/zencoder/content/dam/autodesk/www/products/autodesk-maya-lt/video/send-to-unity-fbx-export-video-1280x720.mp4`).

Maya is also an industry standard for 3D artists, and it is supported by both Windows and OS X (while 3D Studio Max, for example, isn't). You can check out 3D forums to delve into the differences between 3D software. The following is a list of very popular forums to begin with:

- `http://forums.cgsociety.org/`
- `http://www.polycount.com/forum/`
- `http://www.gameartisans.org/forums/forum.php`

Setting up a scene in Maya

The first point to keep in mind when setting up a scene in Maya is that the standard unit in Maya is 1 cm, while the standard unit in Unity is 1 m So, whenever you export an FBX file from Maya into Unity, Unity scales it down to 0.01 percent of its original size.

Another very relevant point is that Maya and Unity are affected by strange kinds of idiosyncrasies that put them on opposing sides, with regard to what left or right and front or bottom mean. This is not something that only happens between Maya and Unity. Many 3D software disagree about the concepts of right and up. To get an idea, have a look at the following image, taken from Unity's forum:

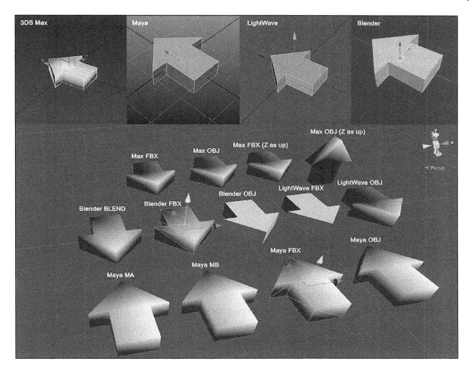

As you can see, the red arrow, representing the left-right axis in the 3D world, may point to the left or right on different software or file formats, and the green and blue axes may switch to alternatively point to the forward or upward directions.

With Maya and Unity, what happens is that the front in Maya is the back in Unity. So you model the front of a character in Maya, and when you import it into Unity, it shows its back.

How do we deal with this? There's more than one option available, and turning the camera by 180 degrees in Unity is not the only one. We will show you how to deal with this problem but, before this, we need to learn how to actually export an FBX file from Maya and add it to a Unity scene, which is what we will do in the first recipe of this chapter.

Getting ready

For this recipe, we need a Maya scene with a 3D model, any model with at least one material applied to it. A textured model is provided with the contents of this book.

How to do it...

In this recipe, we will show you how a model is exported from Maya using the default FBX exporter panel and how the FBX file will get imported in Unity.

1. Open your model in Maya.

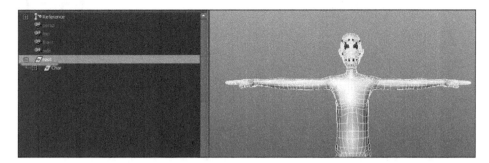

2. Open the outliner panel, and from the hierarchy, select the root node of your model. Remember that it is good practice to name the root node with a meaningful name, such as root. It can turn out to be useful, for example, when managing the exporting process through scripts (as shown later).

3. Now, in the top menu window, navigate to **File** | **Export Selection**. The Maya exporter panel will open, as shown in the following screenshot. Don't bother with the panel on the right-hand side with the actual settings; we will get back to it in a while.

4. Be sure that **FBX export** is selected from the drop-down menu at the bottom.

5. Put a name you like in the **File name** field.

6. Click on **Export Selection** to save the file in your destination folder.

7. Now open Unity and, in the project panel, right-click and select **Import New Asset....** from the menu:

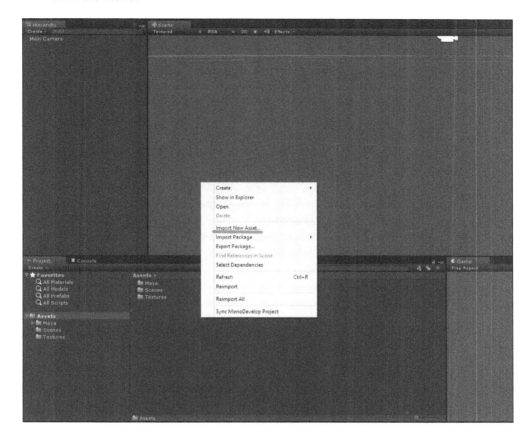

8. Select your saved FBX file from the **Explorer** window that opens and click on **Import**.

9. Alternatively, you could have directly exported the FBX file from Maya into the Assets/Models directory of your Unity project.

10. Now select the FBX file from the project panel and drag it onto the scene. The following screenshot shows what happens in Unity:

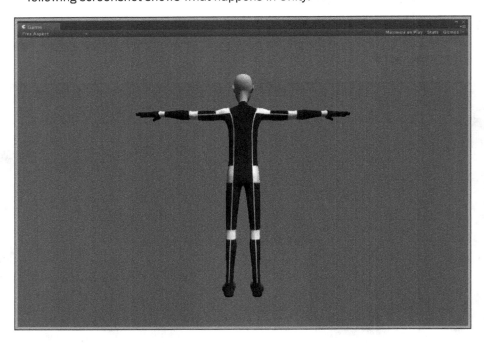

How it works...

The operation of exporting FBX files from Maya is simple: select the actual root node in the hierarchy and click on the **Export** button. But, as you can see, unless we use some precautions, the result of importing an FBX file from Maya is that the model is flipped by 180 degrees on the the y axis in Unity. This happens because the blue arrow that represents the z axis in Maya points in the opposite direction in Unity. As a consequence, the model shows its back to Unity's camera.

As we write, there are rumors that this issue is going to be solved in forthcoming Unity versions. For now, we will provide custom solutions we have used ourselves.

Using groups to rotate FBX files

An efficient solution to dealing with the discrepancy between Maya and Unity is to act on Maya's side and rotate the model on its y axis there. Though, as we write, this problem is going to be solved soon by Maya LT, we offer a solution here that prevents the imported FBX file from acting strangely once they are turned into prefabs in Unity. The idea is to use the so-called "groups" to apply the transformations required and yet get a clean hierarchy for the prefab to appear in Unity. Let's see how to do it.

Getting ready

Open the scene again with the model we used before and be ready to follow our instructions.

How to do it...

In this recipe, we will show you how to use groups and hierarchies in Maya to export a model that will not show its back once it gets imported into Unity. Have the Maya scene open on your screen.

1. From the outliner panel, select the **root** node of your model. Be sure that the model is at the 0,0,0 position with 0,0,0 rotation.

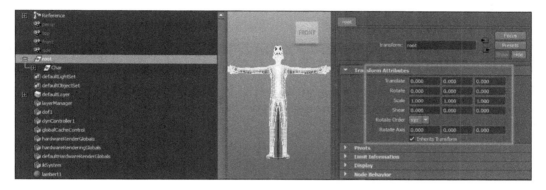

2. With **root** node selected, press *Ctrl+G* to create a group in the hierarchy.
3. Double-click on the newly created group name to edit it and type `rot_180` (this is actually just for reference so we know what the group means).
4. Set a value, namely 180, for the rotation on the *y* axis in the **Transform Attributes** panel.
5. With the `rot_180` group selected in the hierarchy, press *Ctrl+G* again to create another group. Name this group `export` after double-clicking on the group name in the hierarchy.
6. Now you can select the **export** node to export the selection in order to get an FBX file out of this model.

How it works...

By using one group for flipping the model on the *y* axis and another to make a selection featuring neither rotations nor translations for the export, we made sure that the FBX file won't have any unexpected rotation or position offsets that will affect its behavior once it gets scripted into the code in Unity.

There's more...

Another technique we will only mention here is to use your programming skills and code an `AssetPostprocessor` class to handle the process automatically.

`AssetPostprocessor` is a class in Unity, provided with several methods to act on the pipeline for importing assets into Unity.

What one could do is add a custom attribute to the model in Maya, something like turn me 180 degrees on the *y* axis when imported, and let the `AssetPostprocessor` class read this attribute and perform the transformation.

You can learn more about the `AssetPostprocessor` class by checking the scripting reference guide at `http://docs.unity3d.com/ScriptReference/AssetPostprocessor.html`.

Exporting FBX files from Maya

Now that we are done with our first import, we can approach the many settings available in the Maya FBX exporter panel. There are several operations that require our attention, so follow us in our next recipe.

Getting ready

For this recipe, you just need the Maya model we used so far.

How to do it...

1. Open the scene with the model in Maya.
2. From the outliner panel, select the **root** node of your model. Be sure that the model is at the 0,0,0 position with 0,0,0 rotation.
3. In the top menu window, navigate to **File | Export Selection** and the Maya exporter panel will open.
4. Be sure that **FBX export** is selected from the drop-down menu at the bottom of the panel.
5. Put a name you like in the **File name** field.
6. From the **Options...** panel on the right-hand side, let's examine the first group of settings. Edit the **General Options**, **Reference Options**, and **Include Options** tab, as shown in the following screenshot:

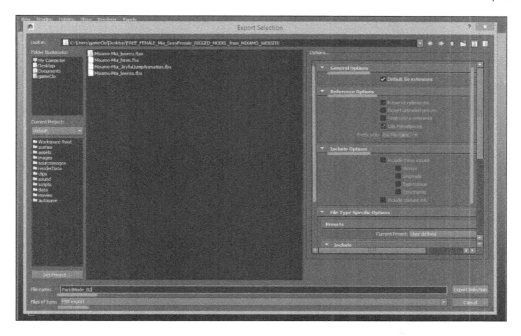

7. Now we can move to the next group of settings. In **File Type Specific Options**, make sure that the **Include** and **Geometry** settings are configured as shown in the following screenshot:

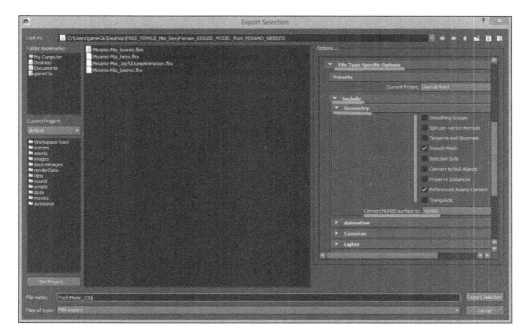

8. Next comes the animation-related group of properties. Since we are not importing animations with an FBX file, unflag the **Animation** option entirely. This action will disengage all the following properties (see that they are barred in the following screenshot).

9. Unflag **Cameras**, **Lights**, and **Embed Media**; we don't need any of them either.

10. Flag **Input Connections** in the **Connections** tab. Refer to the following screenshot for the last three steps:

11. Finally, in the **Advanced Options** tab, check that **Units** is set to **Automatic**.

12. Check that **Axis Conversion** is set to **Up Axis: Y**.

13. Check that **FBX File Format** is set to the latest Maya version available for your Maya installation (Binary **FBX 2014**, as we write). Refer to the following screenshot to be sure you have set everything correctly:

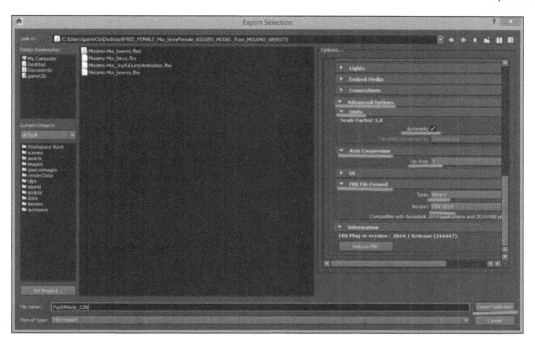

14. Set a `destination` directory for the export, most likely the `Asset\FBX` directory in your Unity project.
15. You can now press **Export Selection** to have the FBX file saved and ready to be used in Unity.

How it works...

As you can see, there is quite a lot that can be tweaked with regard to exporting FBX files from Maya. What we offered here was a basic outline that will do for most cases. It is very likely that, depending on the specific need that would rise with your own project, you may need to use different settings on specific tabs. In such cases, we suggest you to refer to the official Unity documentation, where an entire section dedicated to exporting from Maya is available.

Anyway, at some point, you will have determined the optimal settings configuration for your project and won't need to reset them every time. Once you get your optimal configuration, the only change will be with regard to the **Animation** tab. Don't worry about it now; we'll get to importing animations soon.

There's more...

If you check Unity's reference manuals (`http://docs.unity3d.com/Manual/HOWTO-ImportObjectMaya.html`), you may learn that Unity actually imports native Maya files, which means you can directly open Maya scenes (`*.mb` and `*.ma` files) in Unity. You can therefore ask, Why export FBX files into Unity at all?

There is more than one reason actually; one that is worth $4,000 is that FBX files are far more shareable than native Maya files. For example, to open a Maya scene in Unity, you must have Maya installed or the file won't open. If you expect to exchange files between people on their own PCs, you cannot assume that each one of them will have a Maya license. It will thus be safer to use formats that don't require additional costly software, as is the case with Maya (almost $4,000 per license).

That said, it is still quite useful to open Maya scenes in Unity. For example, in Unity you can immediately check the result of modifications made on a file in Maya without the need to export an FBX file with each new edit. Also, as already stated, Maya LT is going to export FBX file directly into Unity.

Configuring imported FBX files in Unity

Whenever an FBX file is imported into Unity, it is possible to edit some of its properties using Unity Inspector. Usually, these are operations that are required for setting things such as the correct scale of the model, the materials settings, as well as animations and other animation-related settings.

The following recipe provides useful hints on correctly specifying these settings using Unity Inspector.

Getting ready

For this recipe, we will basically resume from where we left the previous recipe. After having exported the model from Maya, launch Unity. By default, Unity always opens up to the last project you worked on.

How to do it...

1. From the `FBX` folder in your `Assets` directory, select the FBX file you just imported.
2. In the **Inspector** panel, let's begin with the **Model** tab. Depending on the actual unit system you set Maya with, you may need to set **Scale Factor** for Unity. By default, Unity scales down imported FBX files to one-hundredth of their original size. If you didn't consider this when modeling the object in Maya, you may need to scale it up in Unity Inspector. In our case, we scale the model back to its original size, setting **Scale Factor** to 1.

3. Set both **Normals** and **Tangents** to **Import** from the drop-down menu.

4. Flag the **Import Materials** option.

5. From the drop-down menu, set **Materials Naming** to **From Model's Materials**.

6. For completeness, check that **Material Search** is set to **Recursive-Up**, which is the default setting.

7. Click on the **Apply** button on the bottom-right corner. Check the following screenshot to ensure you did everything right:

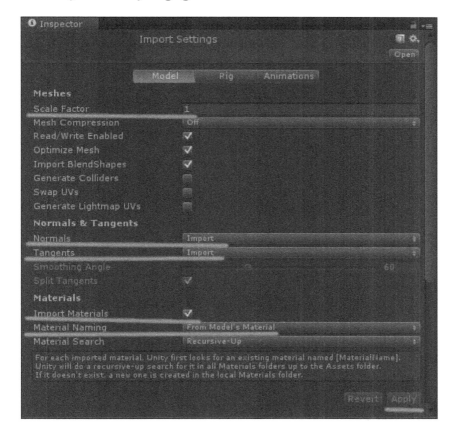

8. We can now move to the next tab, **Rig**. In the **Avatar Definition** field, select **Create From This Model** from the drop-down menu. This setting is important in order to animate the character. What we are stating here is that we want the **Rig** model for this character to be created from this actual FBX file.

9. In the **Root node** field, set the `root` node of your model, then click on **Apply**. Check the following screenshot for reference. As stated previously, we took care of naming our root node `root` earlier:

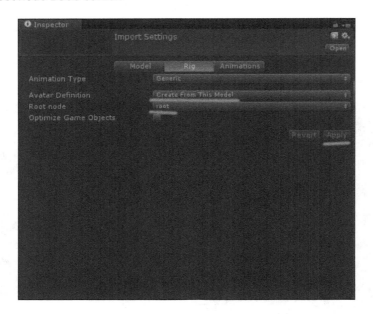

10. The last tab is called **Animations**. Since we are not importing the animations of our model with this specific FBX file, we will unflag the **Import Animation** option, as shown in the following screenshot:

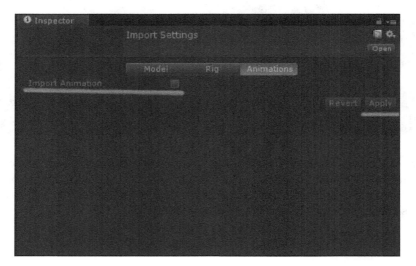

11. Click on **Apply** to update the setting.

How it works...

As already said with regard to the export settings in Maya, what we provided here was a default reference to set an FBX file imported in Unity. You may need to change some of these settings based on specific matters related to how you modeled your object in Maya and\or how you exported and\or planned to use it as a Unity game object.

We suggest you experiment with **Inspector** settings to get a wider grasp of the meaning of each setting and refer to the Unity documentation available at `http://docs.unity3d.com/Manual/HOWTO-exportFBX.html` when you have questions.

Exporting animations

It is very likely that models are enriched with animations to improve the quality of their behavior as game objects. In the following recipe, we will see how to export animations from Maya.

Getting ready

When exporting animations, two approaches are possible. One, which we will adopt in this book, is to keep things on separate files. With this approach, we export one FBX file for the model, the materials, and the rigging (as we did before), and one FBX file for each individual animation, such as idle, run, jump, and the like.

The other approach is to export everything on a single file. In this case, the exported FBX file will consist of the model, materials, rigging, and a timeline containing the frames for the entire animation set of the character. We will discuss this second approach later.

As usual, we took care of providing the required assets (animated Maya scenes for the model) in case you don't have any.

How to do it...

1. With the root node of the animated model selected in the outliner, navigate to **File | Export Selection** as usual.

2. Select **FBX File Format** in the exporting panel and name your file. If you want Unity to automatically read the animation name when it is imported, follow the official naming convention that requires the animation file to be named `modelName@animationName` (with @ before the animation name). Assuming that we are about to export the **idle** animation for our character, name the file `modelName@idle`.

3. Select the `destination` directory for the `Animation` file, which should be under **Animations** in your Unity project.

4. In the **Options...** panel, we need to make some adjustments to import the animation correctly. Under the **Animation** tab, flag the **Animation** option.

5. In the **Bake Animation** field, check that **Bake Animation** is flagged and that the starting and ending frame for the current animation are selected (this should be done automatically by Maya).

6. In the **Deformed Models** field, check that all the flags are selected. These settings may change, depending on the specific requirements of each individual model and animation set.

7. You don't need to change anything else with regard to the setting we defined to export the static model, so you can click on **Export Selection**.

How it works...

As we will see in the following recipe, where we will edit the settings of the imported animation in Unity, what we get is an FBX file containing an animation clip named `idle`, which represents the idle animation for our character.

As we said before, it is possible to trace the animation clips on a single file\timeline and export all character animations in one FBX file; in this case, however, additional operations are required when compared to the one-file-one animation technique.

With a single file containing all the clips, Unity is not capable, by default, to read the timeline imported from Maya and automatically detecting the individual clips, and you end up with a single, most likely long, timeline named `track01` containing all the animations.

So you have to split the whole timeline by yourself, naming each clip individually and manually setting the start and end frames for each one of them in Unity Inspector.

If you think about a typical working pipeline with different people taking care of different operations, you may find your animators manually writing a text file of some sort with information regarding animation clip names and their reference frames. The animators then pass on this text file to someone responsible for taking care of importing animations in Unity. This last guy would also be responsible for typing the data found in the text file into Unity Inspector. A way of doing things that can easily lead to human errors, as you can imagine...

This is the reason why we prefer using separate FBX files for each animation clip.

It is also possible to automate the exporting process so it doesn't become a time-consuming activity, but you may need a programmer for this.

The idea is to script a piece of code in MEL to handle the job. MEL is the scripting scaffold of Maya: any operation you perform in the Maya editor has an equivalent instruction in MEL. Since performing hardcoding in the MEL scripting language would go beyond the scope of this book, we just provide a few references here for those interested. The list of MEL exporting commands is available at `http://download.autodesk.com/us/fbx/20112/Maya/_index.html`.

An example MEL script, courtesy of James Kyle, is available at

`http://www.jameskyle.net/2013/03/maya-to-fbx-batch-export/`.

There's more...

For those of you who are interested in automating the exporting process, there are ways, pretty elegant too, that require advanced programming skills.

One way is to create a **Maya Embedded Language** (**MEL**) script that reads the scene in Maya and exports what you need, based on the settings you define for the exporting process. MEL is the programming language behind Maya; any operation performed in Maya can be converted into a scripting instruction that will achieve exactly the same result. By using MEL, you can thus create a script that automatically exports animation clips into Unity on one or more FBX files, helping you save time (and reduce the risk of errors).

Another option is to configure Maya to generate an XML file that describes the animation data stored in the timeline of a model (animation names, starting\ending frames, and the like), and then read this XML file from Unity to automatically create the required FBX files.

Both these approaches are very similar to using the post-processor to read custom attributes from Maya, as we discussed earlier.

If you'd like to go that way, you can refer to the following links:

► `http://download.autodesk.com/global/docs/maya2014/en_us/index.html?url=files/GUID-312387EC-2907-40D6-A0ED-1BE322106BBB.htm,topicNumber=d30e68424`

► `http://forum.unity3d.com/threads/saving-and-loading-data-xmlserializer.85925/`

Configuring imported animations in Unity Inspector

Before we end this chapter about Maya and Unity, there is one last step we must take care of configuring imported animations in Unity Inspector. This is the topic of our next recipe.

Getting ready

Again, we pick up from where we left the previous lesson. Open Unity and select the animated FBX file in the project panel.

How to do it...

1. With the animated **FBX** file selected in the project panel, go to **Inspector** and access the **Model** tab. Since we are only interested in the animation data stored in this file, we will basically unflag most of the options that we set when we imported the static model. Use the following screenshot as a reference and then click on **Apply**:

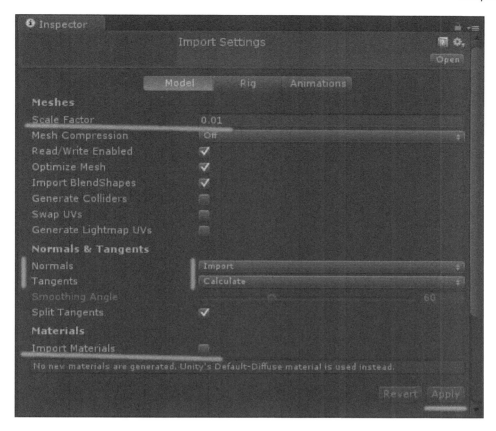

2. Now we move on to the **Rig** tab. As the animation clip stored in this file is to be used by the model we imported before, we need to set the **Avatar Definition** field as **Copy From Other Avatar**.

3. We also need to set the source avatar. Click on the small button to the right of the **Source** field and add the avatar created from the static model to it, as shown in the following screenshot:

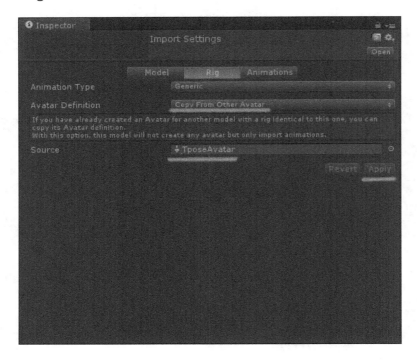

4. Click on **Apply** and select the last tab, **Animations**.

5. In this tab, there is much to do. First of all, flag the **Import Animations** option, which will make a group of related options that depend on this option visible:

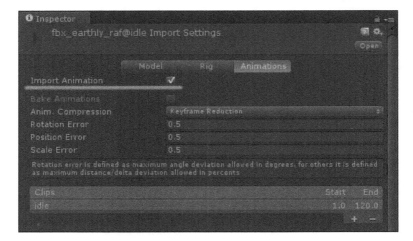

6. Scroll down the panel and look for the **Root Transform Rotation**. Flag **Bake Into Pose** and select **Root Node Rotation** from the drop-down menu.

7. In the **Root Transform Position (Y)** group, flag **Bake Into Pose** and check that **Root Node Position (Y)** is flagged. In the **Root Transform Position (XZ)** group, flag **Bake Into Pose** and ensure that **Root Node Position** isn't flagged.

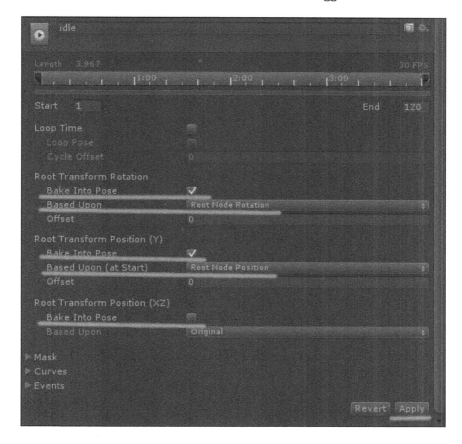

8. Notice that this is an idle animation and, as such, it should be set on looping by flagging the **Loop Time** option. We didn't do this intentionally to provide a more general example.

9. Click on **Apply** to end configuring the animation.

How it works...

Let's begin with a few words on the topic of root motion, as Unity Inspector displays several options about it.

Root motion has to do with controlling the actual position of the mesh with regard to its collider while animations are being played. Most animations happen in place, meaning that the mesh and the collider don't actually move around as the character is animated. This may be the case for examples of walk and run animations.

There are other animations though that require the mesh and collider to actually move or rotate in the 3D world as the animation is played. Actions such as strafing, jumping, and other in-game specials require the mesh and the collider to change their position and rotation in the 3D world as the animation is performed.

By setting the properties of Root Rotation and Root Position groups, you control whether the collider should rotate or move with the mesh during specific animation clips.

In a walk animation, the start and stop root orientations and positions in world space are identical. In such cases where animations are acknowledged by Unity with a green light in Unity Inspector, it is recommended to flag the **Bake Into Pose** option in the **Root Transform Rotation** group and set **Root Node Rotation** from the drop-down menu. Also, flag **Bake Into Pose** in the **Root Transform Position (Y)** group and set **Root Node Position** from the menu.

As for the **Root Transform Position (XZ)** group of options, the manual recommends using them for long, idle animations, where the repetition of many frames could lead the mesh to drift from its collider in the long run. In such cases, it is recommended that you bake the position on the *x* and *z* axes as well.

Latin speakers used to say "Repetita iuvant," meaning repetition helps. The settings provided here are to be intended as general, default settings that may not fit into any situation. For example, you may find yourself having to set **Scale Factor** in the **Model** tab for the animated FBX file too in order to prevent the animation from not fitting the model rig. Alternatively, you may need to tweak the **Root Transform Rotation** and **Root Transform Position** settings differently, depending on how you rigged\animated your model with specific animation clips. As usual, we recommend that you refer to the Unity documentation at `http://docs.unity3d.com/Manual/AnimationsImport.html` whenever you have questions.

There's more...

The **Rig** tab in Unity Inspector displays an option that we didn't mention here: **Animation Type**. You configure this option to select whether you want your character to be animated as a humanoid or a generic object, as it could be with a vehicle, a ball, or whatever.

Also, when a rigged FBX file is imported into a project, Unity automatically creates a so-called avatar out of it. This task is generally performed automatically by Mecanim, the built-in tool responsible for animation setting and management; we will discuss this in detail in *Chapter 3, Animating a Game Character*.

Mecanim has routines that examine the skeletal configuration of a rigged model imported in Unity and then recompute it into a general template it can interpret. This template is called the avatar. Once an avatar has been created, other animation clips can be targeted to that same avatar. This is how multiple animation clips are linked to a single character model in Unity.

In the recipe, we configured the model scale and material in the **Model** tab only for the static version of the model; in the **Rig** tab, we set the **Avatar Definition** option to **Create for this model**. For animated clips, on the other hand, we didn't configure the **Model** tab, and we set **Avatar Definition** to **Copy From Other Avatar** with a reference to the static avatar. This assumes Mecanim succeeds in interpreting the rigged model.

There are cases where for some reason Mecanim is unable to correctly compute the avatar; alternatively, you may just want to make changes on your own. In such cases, it is possible to manually edit the avatar in Unity Inspector and check that all bones required by Mecanim are correctly named and in place.

A recipe about setting up the avatar would go beyond the scope of this book, as it has a lot to do with modeling and rigging techniques, which are beyond the scope of this book.

Refer to the Unity manual at `http://docs.unity3d.com/Manual/AvatarCreationandSetup.html`. Besides this, if you are interested in delving more into this matter, we suggest the many tutorials available on websites about game development and 3D graphics. For example, digital tutors offer many exceptional tutorials about Unity in general and Mecanim in particular; we recommend you check them out.

2
2D Assets for Unity

In this chapter, we will cover the following recipes:

- ▸ Importing textures and setting them to Inspector
- ▸ Configuring transparency
- ▸ Creating materials
- ▸ Setting materials' names in Maya
- ▸ Setting the ambient light in Unity
- ▸ Texture atlases
- ▸ Animated materials

Introduction

Whether your game is going to be 2D or 3D, you will deal with a number of 2D assets, mainly textures. Therefore, before building a game, I will cover this topic and explain how textures and other 2D assets are dealt within Unity.

Though we assume you are familiar with texturing-related matters and image file formats used for texturing games, we are going to describe the most relevant aspects of the operations throughout this chapter.

Some could say that textures should have been covered before importing 3D models into Unity. As a matter of fact, when you export a model from a 3D editor like Maya, the exporting process takes care of setting references between the exported model, its material, and the textures for those materials. Once the model is imported, the material instances are recreated in Unity; if the textures for those materials have already been imported into the project, the materials can actually be read by Unity and the model will (almost) look like it did in Maya.

If the textures have not been imported onto the other side, Unity will miss the references and the model will be displayed with a strong, unnatural, and pink diffused color.

If this is what you ended up with using the recipes described in *Chapter 1, Importing 3D Models and Animations*, then you just need to go through this chapter and reimport the models after the textures.

We decided to treat models before textures because it made sense to us to deal with models first and then deal with the textures for the materials to be applied to those models.

We hope it didn't cause too much trouble!

About textures and materials

Textures are 2D images that go into the materials that are applied to 3D models. They are responsible for the fine details featured by models: colors, bumps, reflections, and other features of the so-called skin of a 3D model.

Materials, on the other hand, can be considered as the actual skin of the 3D model; imagine it as a kind of very elastic and flexible coat that entirely covers the model geometry. Now assume that you can selectively paint this coat so it displays all the details of clothes, be it a suit, a tuxedo, fur, or whatever fits the game design.

This skin is versatile enough that artists can actually add many features to it to reproduce the effect of light bouncing on its surface, thus allowing some parts to look like leather and others like fur, metal, or a piece of a cartoon—anything you can think of.

This characteristic of materials is the result of a computation performed by a graphic program called a shader. A shader is a piece of code that defines how light interacts with the color and other characteristics of a surface in a game scene.

In case you need a summary of what we are saying here, we recommend you check out the interesting article at: `http://www.informit.com/articles/article.aspx?p=2162089&seqNum=2`.

From a quantitative point of view, a single 3D model usually requires more than one material (usually two) and a single material usually requires a couple textures; that's why the `Assets/Textures` folder in a Unity project is very likely to be the largest folder of the entire project!

File formats of textures

As a game requires a lot of textures, it is important to consider how to effectively manage them from a memory-management perspective. Indie and mobile game development (the reference business models we keep in mind as we write this book) especially require you to optimize memory management, as the overall weight of a game in bytes can become a decisive point for its popularity. The following section provides a few rules and hints for using textures in Unity.

Though images come in a different number of file formats in any range from very light to very heavy, when working on an indie project in Unity, it is very likely that you turn to just a couple of them. From Version 4.0, Unity supports PSD files, the native Photoshop file format. That means you can work on an image in Photoshop and then save it directly into a Unity scene. As we stated in *Chapter 1, Importing 3D Models and Animations*, when discussing Unity supporting native Maya files, this is a handy feature to speed up the process of exporting textures into Unity. Just remember that PSD files are flattened upon importing, so you only get the upper layer of the PSD file you save in Unity. On the other hand, the original PSD file in Photoshop won't be affected, so you can keep working on it and take advantage of layers.

The other very popular file type is PNG. PNG files are very light, so you can save memory and also store the information about image transparency. As such, they are used to create transparent materials. Another very good thing of PNG files is that it isn't a proprietary format and you can export and import PNG files with any 2D editor!

Unity supports many file formats, namely TIFF, Targa, and BMP. Discussing all of them goes beyond the scope of this chapter (and this entire fookbook, too!), so we won't go there. You can refer to this link to Wikipedia to start your own research in this field: http://en.wikipedia.org/wiki/Image_file_formats.

Finally, don't worry if you don't have an image library of your own; as usual, we provide the images required for the recipes of this chapter!

Optimizing textures

When preparing textures for a Unity project, there are a number of good practices that are recommended and a couple of rules that must be followed.

First of all, texture sizes should come in powers of two. A reasonable sequence of image sizes in pixels for games made today is 256, 512, 1024, 2048, 4096.

It is not mandatory that textures are square, too, though Unity kindly appreciates that! Whenever you can use square images, do it.

What Unity doesn't like at all, on the other hand, is textures larger than 4096 pixels; if you try to import an image that is larger than 4096 pixels on any of its dimensions, it will automatically reduce to a more comfortable size, most likely 1024 x 1024. Simply, the software doesn't allow you to set an image larger than 4096 pixels. On the other hand, you shouldn't worry about that; 4096 is a very high resolution image and it is more than enough for any (indie or mobile) game.

Many other techniques are available to game artists to optimize graphic performances while reducing the overall memory allocation. Mipmapping, for example, is a technique that improves performance. Using normal maps to improve the look of low-poly models is another. We suggest you research these topics if they are not familiar to you. This link from Wikipedia should provide you with everything you need to know about them: `http://en.wikipedia.org/wiki/Texture_mapping`.

Well then. Assuming you are clear with what we have discussed so far, let's jump into the core of this chapter and start importing textures into our Unity project.

Importing textures and setting them to Inspector

Importing textures into a Unity project is a fundamental activity, and you will perform it several times. The following recipe explains two ways to import textures into Unity and how to configure them for the materials of your 3D models.

Getting ready

For this recipe, you need any square texture that you may already have, or use the one we provide. Anything will do, even a simple, checker texture; there are many available online. We use the following image for this recipe:

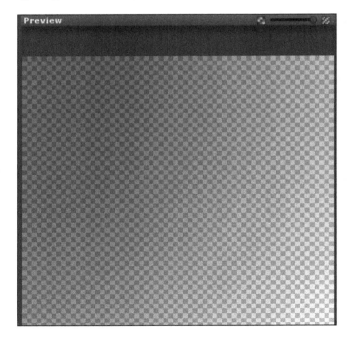

How to do it...

To import a texture in Unity, we begin with opening it into a 2D editor:

1. Open a PSD texture with Photoshop, or the alternative BMP file with any software you like. If you don't have the required software, you can download XnView, which can read PSD files. It is available at `http://www.xnview.com/`.

2. Name the file. We picked the name `firstTexture`.

3. Select the `Assets/Textures` destination folder in your Unity project.

4. Save the file. You can either leave it in its PSD original format or change it into a PNG file. The following screenshot shows how to perform the operation of saving the image as a PSD file:

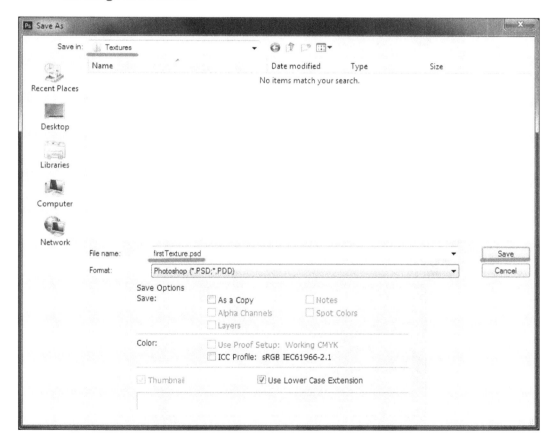

5. The following screenshot, on the other hand, shows how to save it as a PNG file instead:

6. Now launch Unity. From the project panel, select our `firstTexture` PSD file.

7. Access **Inspector** and check that it is set as shown in the following image:

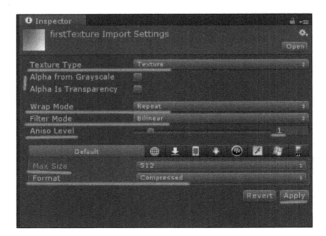

8. Click on the **Apply** button to end this process. The following image shows how the texture preview should look:

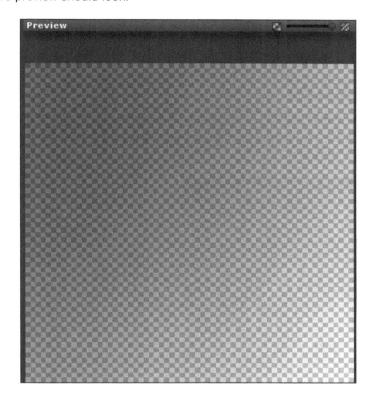

How it works...

Unity allows several texture types to be configured, depending on the use you expect to make of textures for your project. For this recipe, we configured a simple diffuse texture. In the next recipe, we will show you how to deal with transparent textures instead.

Configuring transparency

It is very common to have images that display transparency to add details and improve the look of 3D models. PNG files store the information regarding the alpha channel of an image, so that parts of the image itself can be displayed as transparent. The following recipe shows you how to configure a transparent texture in Unity.

Getting ready

For this recipe, we use another image we have provided, the one named `secondTexture`. As this image is already saved in PNG format, we jump straight into Unity and import it from there.

How to do it...

1. From the **Project** panel in Unity, select the `Assets/Textures` folder.

2. Right-click anywhere and select **Import New Assets**, as shown in the following screenshot:

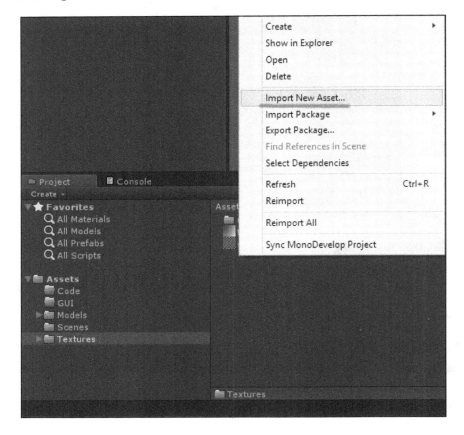

3. Select the **secondTexture** image to upload it into Unity. Actually, Unity is flexible enough that you can even simply copy and paste assets from one folder to another.

4. From the **Inspector** window, check that the texture settings are defined as in the following screenshot:

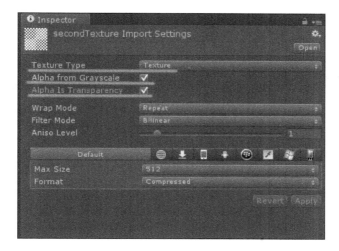

5. Click on **Apply** to save the settings we defined. The following screenshot shows the result:

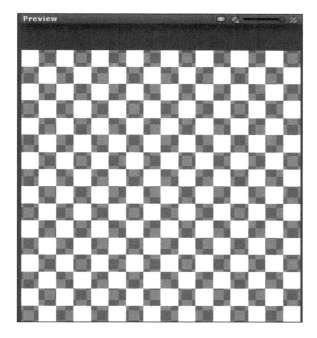

How it works...

This time, in the **Inspector** window, we flagged the options to use the grayscale of the image to display its darkest parts as transparent. As a result, all black squares in the image aren't rendered when this texture goes into a material.

Many other types are available: normal maps, sprites, reflection maps, and GUI elements. In the following recipe, we'll create two distinct materials with the textures we just imported.

Creating materials

As we said, materials are the skin of a model and provide its distinctive look. In the following recipe, we will create two materials that show the difference between a diffuse and transparent material.

Getting ready

As we add an entirely new type of asset to our project in this recipe (didn't we tell you that we were going to create many?), we need to create a folder to store our materials. Open Unity and get ready to follow the instructions of the next recipe!

How to do it...

1. From the **Project** panel, select the `Assets` folder, then click anywhere and select **Create | Folder**, as shown in the following screenshot:

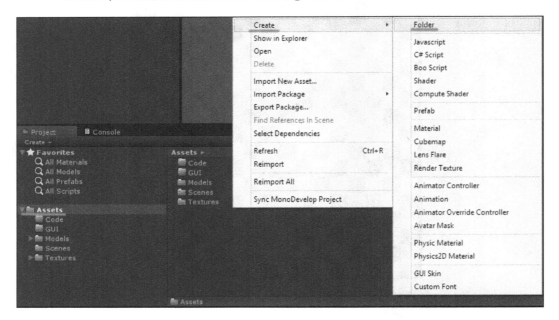

2. Name the folder `Materials`, then double-click to open it.

3. Right-click anywhere on the panel and select **Create | Material**, as shown in the following screenshot:

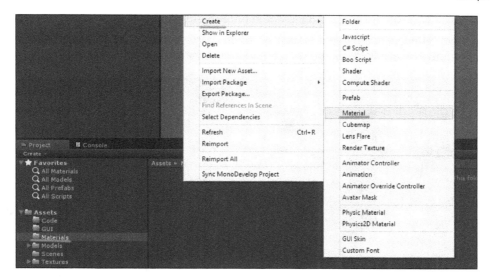

4. Name the material as `filled`, then repeat this operation to create another material and name it `Transparent`. At this point, you should have two gray materials in your `Materials` folder, one named `filled` and the other named `Transparent`.

5. Select `filled`. In **Inspector**, check that **Shader** is set to **Texture** under **Unlit**. This way, our materials won't be affected by light and will simply shine.

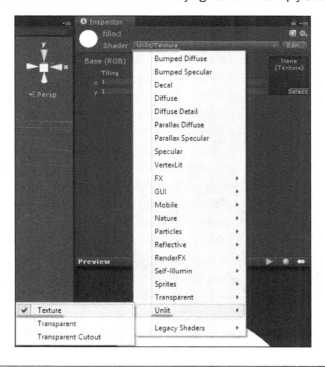

6. Click once on the `Textures` folder in the **Project** panel.

7. With **filled** selected in the **Inspector** window, drag and drop **firstTexture** onto the empty **Texture** field, as shown in the following screenshot:

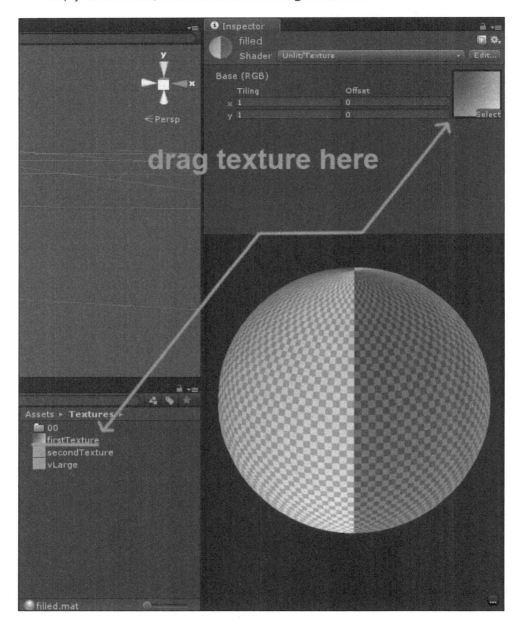

8. Now select **transparent** and repeat the dragging operation with **secondTexture**.

9. This time, check that the **Shader** field is set to **Unlit/Cutout**, as shown in the following screenshot:

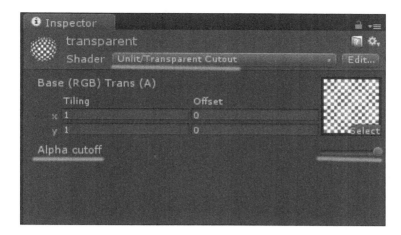

10. You can act on the **Alpha cutoff** slider to adjust the transparency of the black squares on the checker texture, from null to total. The following screenshot shows how the material preview should look:

11. Add two cubes to your scene. This can be done by navigating to **GameObject |
    Create Other** from the top menu, as shown in the following screenshot:

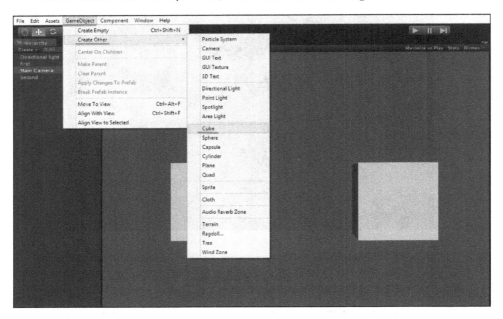

12. Duplicate the cube or create another so that you end up with two cubes in the
    scene. We don't need to add a light to our scene, as we set out materials as
    Unlit, which means they are not actually affected by light at all.

13. Now drag the material named **filled** onto one cube and **transparent** onto the other.
    The following screenshot shows the result you should get:

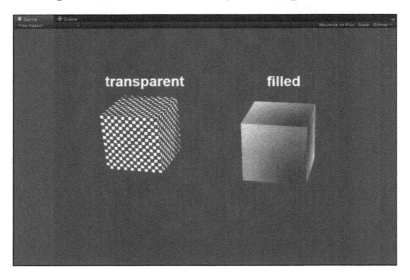

How it works...

By getting the info about transparency from the grayscale of **secondTexture** and setting **transparent** as an **Unlit/Transparent Cutout** material, we caused the checkered cube to appear empty where the dark squares were.

There's more...

Unity offers the possibility to define several other material types, allowing the use of normal and specular maps and many other effects to improve the look of your models. A detailed analysis of all such materials would go beyond the scope of this chapter about importing 2D assets, so we will stop here. We will delve more into materials in the later chapters.

Setting materials' names in Maya

When Unity imports a model, it also imports the materials linked to the model in the 3D editor. By default, the materials are named based on the names of the textures used in the 3D editor to build them.

If you remember from the previous chapter, upon importing a model into Unity, we set an option in the **Model** tab to pick material names from a model's materials, instead of the texture names. Refer to the following screenshot to checkout what we did in *Chapter 1, Importing 3D Models and Animations*:

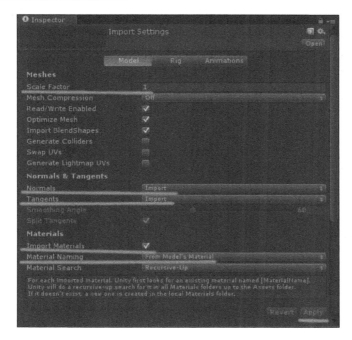

We adopt this solution because it helps keep our project clean and has each asset named correctly. As our goal is to have the materials named with a meaningful convention that can help us keep materials and their textures well separated, in the following recipe, we'll show you how to add custom names to materials in Maya, to be exported into Unity.

Getting ready

For this recipe, we need a textured model to be opened in Maya. Use your own models or the ones we have provided with this book.

How to do it...

1. Open Maya or your 3D editor of choice, then open the model file in the editor.
2. From the main menu, navigate to **Window | RenderingEditors | Hypershade** to open **Hypershade**, the panel where materials and their properties are displayed.
3. Select a material in **Hypeshade** to display its properties in the **Attribute Editor** panel.
4. In the text field, type a name you want to assign to that material. Refer to the following screenshot to check whether you are in the right panel/text field:

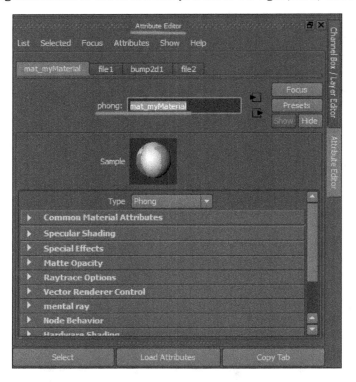

5. Click on **Enter** to save your edits.

How it works...

When this model is exported into Unity and the materials' naming property is correctly set in **Inspector**, a `Materials` folder will be automatically created to store the materials named with the convention we set in Maya.

A drawback of this practice is that you end up with two instances of each material: one named `tex_TexName`, which is automatically created by Unity, and another named `mat_matName`, which is the name you get from applying the settings to the **Inspector** window. You can simply follow this rule: materials whose name starts with `tex*` must be deleted from the project.

Setting the ambient light in Unity

Another useful operation we'd like to teach you is how to set the ambient light in your Unity scene so you can quickly check the look of your materials in the game scene without configuring an actual light.

Getting ready

For this recipe, we just need a scene in Unity with a textured model in it.

How to do it...

1. Create a new scene in Unity and drag **textured model** into the scene. Be sure no lights are available in the scene and that the model's material is set to **Diffuse** in the **Inspector** window. With these lighting conditions, the model should look quite dark.

2. From the main menu, navigate to **Edit | RenderSettings**.

3. Now move to **Inspector**. Here, we can set several options for our ambient light. The one we are interested in here is the ambient light color.

4. By default, **Ambient Light** is set to a dark gray. Click on the **Ambient Light** panel to open the **Color** panel, as shown in the following screenshot:

5. Move the cursor to the white portion (the upper-right corner highlighted in red in the screenshot) in the **Color** panel to set **Ambient Light** to **white**. Now your model should look far more lighter than before!

Check out the following screenshot showing the difference between the two settings on the material:

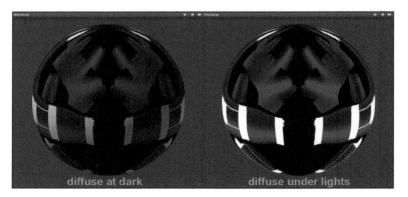

How it works...

The ambient light is a standard illumination setting that defines a homogeneous light coming from all directions, something that only happens in game editors. In the real world, lights always come from a direction and hit objects at angles. As a matter of fact, good lighting has to do specifically with recreating realistic lights for virtual environments, such as games.

Still, setting a useful ambient light can come in handy during the initial phases of game prototyping, before you delve into the matters of actual lighting.

Texture atlases

As we are nearing the end of this chapter, there is one topic we would like to discuss. Let's take a look at the following screenshot, courtesy of Gamasutra:

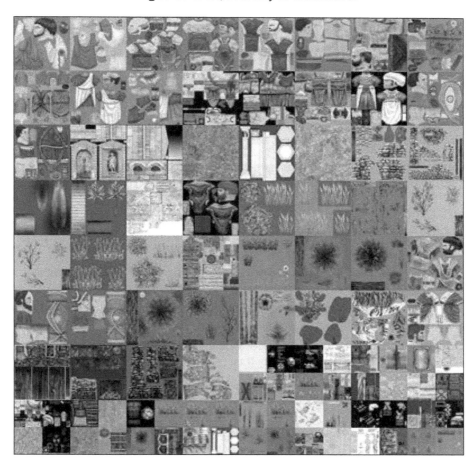

You may notice that it contains an arrangement of images and parts of images that are all nicely deployed to better fill the whole space available. This is technically called a texture atlas. A texture atlas is in fact a way to optimize memory management as you feed your project with 2D textures. Instead of having an image for any differently colored mesh or mesh part, an artist can align several chunks on a single texture, saving memory that would otherwise go wasted.

Actually, in 2D gaming, texture atlases are extremely useful for backgrounds. To improve the perspective illusion of 2D static backgrounds, it is a good practice to actually build them as is done in theaters, by putting several screens on stage at different depths (distance from the audience), each with its own piece of background.

Likewise, artists create pre-rendered backgrounds by putting several images on different planes (or quads, more likely) that they scatter around on the game stage. On each of those quads (quads, by the way, are very simple, single-faced 3D shapes, made of a rectangular plane divided into two triangles), artists put an image selected from a texture atlas, which contains all the images required to actually build up that background. Simple as that!

As it is an important subject for 2D games, in the next recipe, we show how to make a texture atlas from a group of images.

Getting ready

This recipe requires two steps. The first is to create a proper texture atlas using a 2D editor. Our choice is Photoshop, but you can do it with, I believe, any other editor.

The second step happens in Unity, where we configure the texture atlas in **Inspector**. So be ready to open your Unity project, too.

How to do it...

1. Open your 2D editor of choice, ours is Photoshop.

2. Create a new file. This will be our actual atlas, to be filled with other images. If you don't have other images, you can use the ones we have provided.

3. Make the file large, set the file size to 2048 x 2048 pixels, so it is a large texture. A resolution of 72 points should be fine.

4. Set your editor so it displays the reference grid and set the grid to **256 px**. The following screenshot will clarify this:

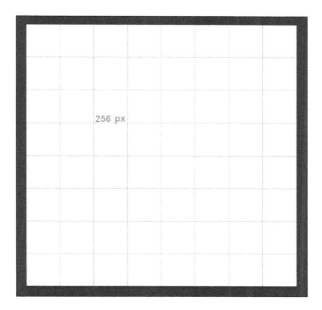

5.   Now you are ready to start importing other images into this grid. In Photoshop, several images can be added as so-called levels to another image. We are pretty sure other software do this as well.

6.   As you import new images, take care when deploying them so each one has its own separate slice of image to occupy. You can use the grid to help you out with this. The following screenshot shows the result we got:

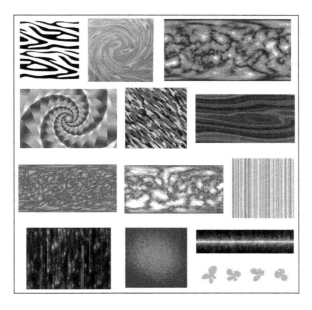

7. Save the texture atlas. Since Unity needs the information about transparency to effectively import the atlas, remove any default background from the original image before saving it as a PNG file.

8. Now switch to Unity. Open the project and create a new folder inside the `Assets\ Textures` folder and name it `Texture Atlas`. We insist on this so your projects are well organized, with different folders for different types of assets.

9. Double-click on the `Texture Atlas` folder to open it, then right-click inside the **Project** panel window and select **Import New Asset**, as we did before.

10. Select the atlas PSD or BMP file in your `destination` folder and click on **Import** to add it to the Unity project.

11. Next, select **Texture Atlas** in the **Project** panel in Unity; we need to set a few properties in **Inspector**.

12. Set **Texture Type** to **Sprite**, **Sprite Mode** to **Multiple**, **Max Size** to **2048** (the size of the original image we made), and **Format** to **Truecolor**. You can refer to the following screenshot:

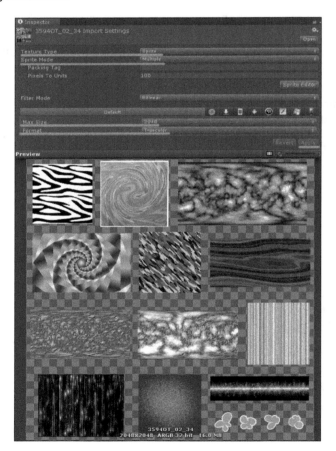

13. Click on **Apply** to save these settings.

14. In **Inspector**, click on the **Sprite Editor** button to open the **Sprite Editor** window, as shown in the following screenshot:

15. In this panel, click on the **Slice** button to open a panel. Check that the settings are the same as those displayed in the following screenshot, then click on **Slice**:

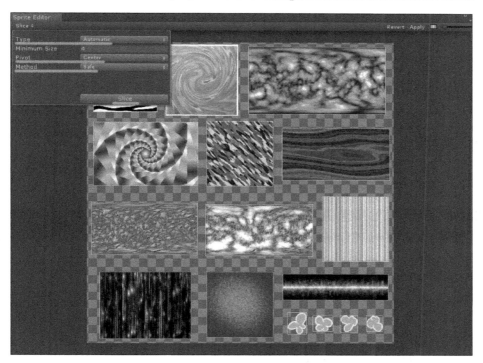

16. If nothing bad happened, you should see a thin white line around each image in the atlas, meaning that Unity has correctly identified and isolated each chunk of the atlas.

How it works...

Though it required several steps, building a texture atlas is quite simple and very useful. The principle is simple: create a large image and fill it with other images. As long as you use a transparent background and leave enough room between each image in the collection, Unity is good enough to slice it up automatically.

About the settings we defined, we set the image as a sprite made out of multiple chunks to allow automatic slicing. Setting the image to a non-compressed format is also required for automatic slicing.

There's more...

There are more settings you can tweak for specific requirements, but we cannot explain all of them here, so we have provided a bunch of useful links about texture atlases and their management in Unity.

The first two are links from Unity manuals about texture settings and the Sprite Editor:

```
http://docs.unity3d.com/Manual/class-TextureImporter.html
```

```
http://docs.unity3d.com/Manual/SpriteEditor.html
```

The next link is a very interesting read about texture atlases from Gamasutra:

```
http://www.gamasutra.com/view/feature/2530/practical_texture_atlases.
php
```

Last is the link to a PDF manual from nVidia corporation about texture optimization, for those of you who really want to dig into this topic:

```
http://http.download.nvidia.com/developer/NVTextureSuite/Atlas_Tools/
Texture_Atlas_Whitepaper.pdf
```

Animated materials

Another very useful thing that can be done with materials is to animate them by manipulating their so called UVs to get interesting rendering effects.

U and V are the letters used to refer to the *x* and *y* axes of a 2D image that is going to be used to texture a 3D mesh. As the X, Y, and Z letters are already in use for the model, the *x* and *y* axes for the image are named with the letters U and V.

The process of putting a 2D image on a 3D model is consequently called UV mapping, and it is a very basic activity for any 3D artist.

As a complete tour of UV mapping would go beyond the scope of this chapter, we suggest you checkout this Wikipedia link to begin learning more about it: `http://en.wikipedia.org/wiki/UV_mappingt`.

The next recipe describes how textures can be animated through code.

Getting ready

For this recipe, we need a texture, a game object, and a piece of code. We provided a nice spiral texture for you to use, in case you don't already have one.

How to do it...

1. Start a new Unity scene.

2. Access the `Assets/Textures` folder and import the image named `spiralTex`, or any other texture of your choice.

3. Create a new material in the `Materials` folder and name it `mat_spiral`.

4. Drag **spiralTex** onto `mat_Spiral` as we did before.

5. Create a `Sphere` in the scene by selecting **GameObject | CreateOther | Sphere** from the main menu.

6. Now drag `mat_spiral` onto the sphere in your scene. The following screenshot shows how the material should look:

7. For the next step, we need a script to be added to our sphere. Let's first create a new folder in our `Assets` directory named `Scripts` to store the new asset (you should remember how to do that from previous recipes).

8. In the `Scripts` folder, create a new `C# script` folder, as shown in the following screenshot:

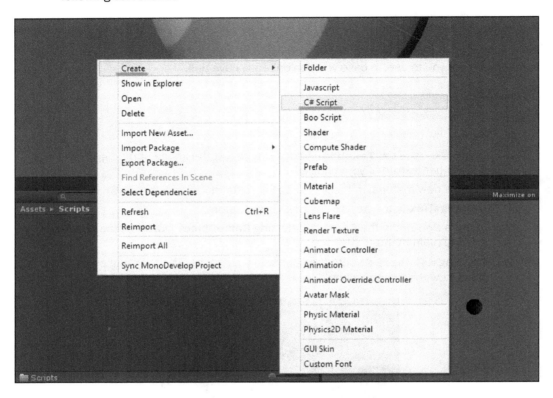

9. Name this script `AnimateUV` and double-click on it to open it in **Monodevelop**, the default Unity script editor.

10. Add the following code to the script:

```
using UnityEngine;
using System.Collections;
public class AnimateUV : MonoBehaviour {
  public float scrollSpeed = 0.5f;
  // Use this for initialization

  // Update is called once per frame
  void Update () {
    float offSetY=scrollSpeed*Time.time;
    myVector = new Vector2(0, offSetY);
    renderer.material.SetTextureOffset("_MainTex", myVector);
  }
}
```

11. Drag the `animateUV` script onto the sphere in the scene and click on the **Play** button. What you should get is the spiral texture rotating around the *y* axis on the game object. Don't fall asleep!

How it works...

With this script, we set a speed for the rotation of the texture (the `scrollSpeed` float variable) and then use time passing by to make the texture rotate on the *y* axis of the model (by multiplying `scrollSpeed` for time).

The instruction to actually rotate the texture UVs is `renderer.material.SetTextureOffset`, which asks for a material component to operate on (in our case, the diffuse component of the material, specified with the `_MainTex` conventional name) and a `Vector2` variable to define rotation on the *x* or *y* axis (or both, if you like). As a matter of fact, in this recipe, we acted on the *y* axis.

There's more...

Though scripting is planned to be the topic of another chapter, we decided to add this recipe here to show you an interesting example of how materials can be manipulated through scripting. To learn more about advanced usage of textures and materials, we recommend you check out the online Unity reference manual at `http://docs.unity3d.com/Manual/Textures.html`.

3
Animating a Game Character

In this chapter, we will cover the following recipes:

- ▶ Creating an animation tree
- ▶ Dealing with transitions
- ▶ Coding the Boolean-based transitions
- ▶ Working with float parameters
- ▶ Coding the float-based transitions
- ▶ Creating Blend Tree
- ▶ Animation layers – creating masks
- ▶ Animation layers – adding a second animation layer

Introduction

Now that we have imported the necessary graphic assets for a prototype, we can approach its actual building in Unity, starting by making an animation set for our character.

Unity implements an easy-to-approach animation system, though quite powerful, called **Mecanim**. Mecanim is a proprietary tool of Unity in which the animation clips belonging to a character are represented as boxes connected by directional arrows. Boxes represent states, which you can simply think of as idle, walk, run...you get the idea.

Arrows, on the other hand, represent the transitions between the states, which are responsible for actually blending between one animation clip and the next. Thanks to transitions, we can make characters that pass smoothly, for example, from a walking animation into a running one.

The control of transitions is achieved through parameters: variables belonging to different types that are stored in the character animator and are used to define and check the conditions that trigger an animation clip. The types available are common in programming and scripting languages: `int`, `float`, and `bool`. A distinctive type implemented in Mecanim is the trigger, which is useful when you want a transition to be triggered as an all-or-nothing event. By the way, an animator is a built-in component of Unity, strictly connected with the Mecanim system, which is represented as a panel in the Unity interface. Inside this panel, the so-called animation tree of a character is actually built-up and the control parameters for the transitions are set and linked to the clips.

Time for an image to help you better understand what we are talking about! The following picture shows an example of an animator of a standard game character:

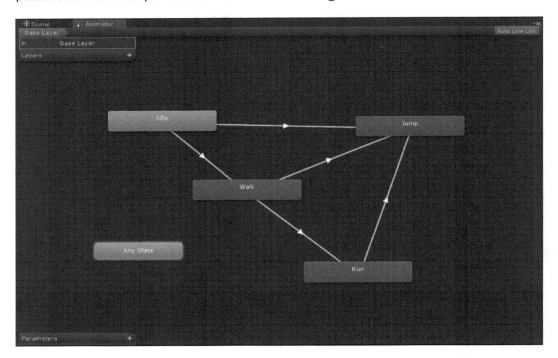

As you can see, there are four states connected by transitions that configure the logic of the flow between one state and another. Inside these arrows, the parameters and their reference values to actually trigger the animations are stored.

With Mecanim, it's quite easy to build the animation tree of a character and create the logic that determines the conditions for the animations to be played. One example is to use a `float` variable to blend between a walking and a running cycle, having the speed of the character as the control parameter. Using a `trigger` or a `boolean` variable to add a jumping animation to the character is another fairly common example. These are the subjects of our following two recipes, starting with trigger-based blending.

We follow on from *Chapter 1, Importing 3D Models and Animations*, where you learned how to import the animation clips for a game character. Follow us!

Creating the animation tree

In this recipe, we show you how to add animation clips to the animator component of a game object (our game character). This being done, we will be able to set the transitions between the clips and create the logic for the animations to be correctly played.

Getting ready

First of all, we need a set of animation clips, imported in Unity and configured in **Inspector**. We explained these operations in *Chapter 1, Importing 3D Models and Animations*, so we suggest going back to it in case you haven't checked that part yet. As usual, we provide the Assets folder you need, in case you don't have your own to use.

Before we proceed, be sure you have these four animation clips imported into your Unity project as FBX files: Char@Idle, Char@Run, Char@Jump, and Char@Walk.

How to do it...

The first operation is to create a folder to store the **Animator Controller**.

1. From the project panel, select the Assets folder and create a new folder for the Animation Controller. Name this folder Animators.

2. In the Animators folder, create a new Animator Controller option by navigating to **Create | Animator Controller**, as shown in the following screenshot:

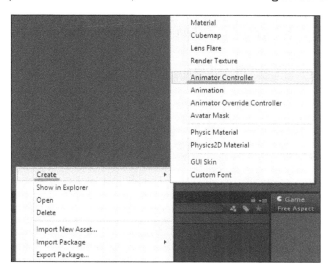

3. Name the asset `Character_Animator`, or any other name you like.

4. Double-click on `Character_Animator` to open the **Animator** panel in Unity. Refer to the following screenshot; you should have an empty grid with a single magenta box called **Any State**:

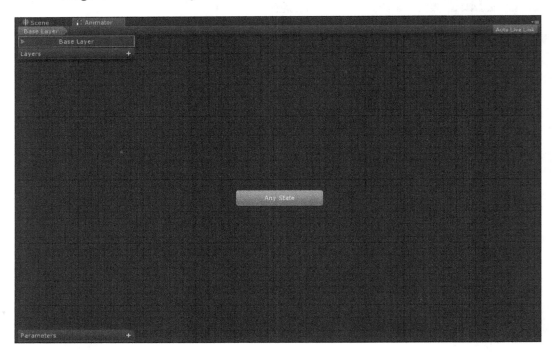

5. Access the `Models/Animations` folder and select `Char@Idle`. Expand its hierarchy to access the actual animation clip named `Idle`; animation clips are represented by small play icons. Refer to the following screenshot for more clarity:

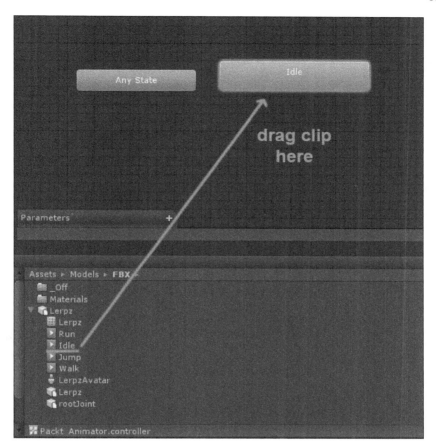

6. Now drag the clip into the **Animator** window. The clip should turn into a box inside the panel (colored in orange to represent that). Being the first clip imported into the **Animator** window, it is assumed to be the default animation for the character. That's exactly what we want!

7. Repeat this operation with the clip named Jump, taken from the Char@Jump FBX file. The following screenshot shows what should appear in the **Animator** window:

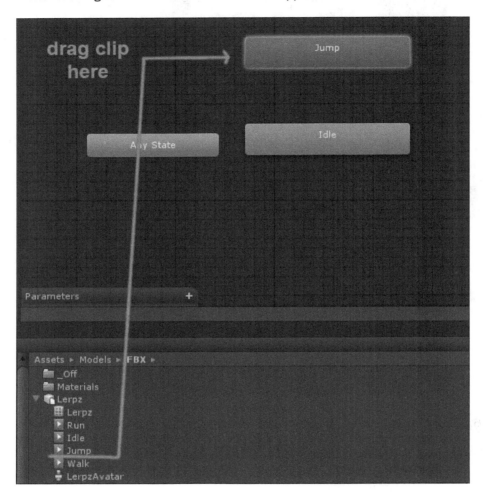

How it works...

By dragging animation clips from the project panel into the **Animator** editor, Mecanim creates a logic state for each of them. As states, the clips are available to connect through transitions and the animation tree of the character can come to life.

With the **Idle** and **Jump** animations added to the **Animator** window, we can define the logic to control the conditions to switch between them.

In the following recipe, we create the transition to blend between these two animation clips.

Dealing with transitions

In this recipe, we create and set up the transition for the character to switch between the **Idle** and **Jump** animation clips. For this task, we also need a parameter, which we will call `bJump`, to trigger the jump animation through code.

Getting ready

We will build on the previous recipe. Have the **Animator** window open, and be ready to follow our instructions.

How to do it...

1. As you move to the **Animator** panel in Unity, you should see a orange box representing the **Idle** animation, from our previous recipe. If it is not, right-click on it, and from the menu, select **Set As Default**. You can refer to the following screenshot:

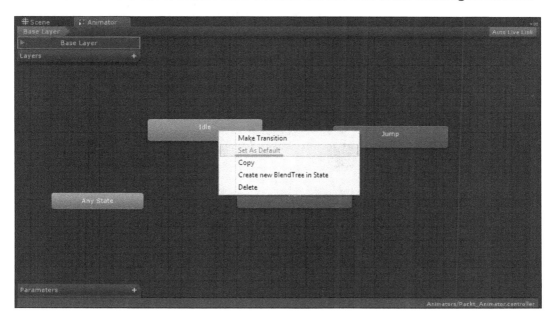

2. Right-click on the **Idle** clip and select **Make Transition** from the menu, as shown in the following screenshot:

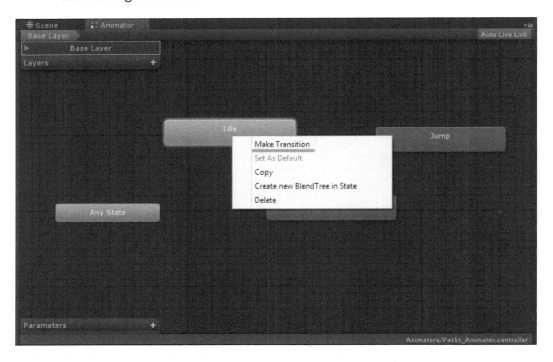

3. Drag the arrow that appears onto the **Jump** clip and click to create the transition. It should appear in the **Inspector** window, to the right of the **Animator** window. Check the following screenshot to see whether you did it right:

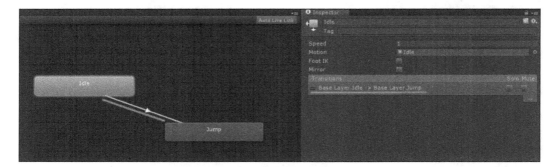

4. Now that we have got the transition, we need a parameter to switch between **Idle** and **Jump**. We use a `boolean` type for this, so we first need to create it. In the bottom-left corner of the **Animator** window, click on the small **+**, and from the menu that appears, select **Bool**, as shown in the following screenshot:

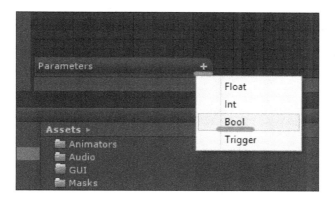

5. Name the newly created parameter `bJump` (the "b" stands for the `boolean` type; it's a good habit to create meaningful variable names).

6. Click on the white arrow representing the transition to access its properties in **Inspector**. There, a visual representation of the transition between the two clips is available.

7. By checking the **Conditions** section in **Inspector**, you can see that the transition is right now controlled by **Exit Time**, meaning that the **Jump** clip will be played only after the **Idle** clip has finished playing. The 0.97 value tells us that the transition is actually blending between the two clips for the last 3 percent of the idle animation. For your reference, you can adjust this value if you want to blend it a bit more or a bit less. Please refer to the following screenshot:

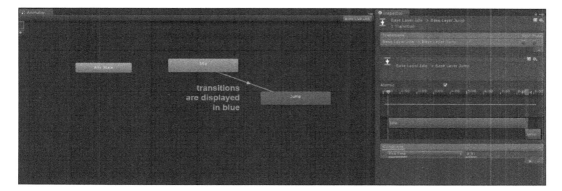

8. As we want our `bJump` parameter to control the transition, we need to change **Exit Time** using the `tJump` parameter. We do that by clicking on the drop-down menu on **Exit Time** and selecting `tJump` from the menu, as shown in the following screenshot:

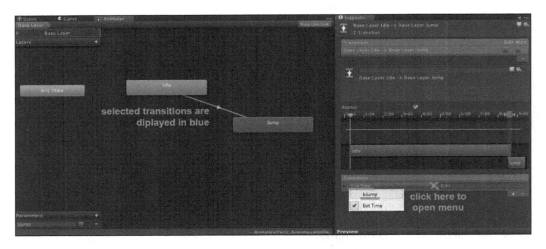

9. Note that it is possible to add or remove conditions by acting on the small **+** and - buttons in the interface if you need extra conditions to control one single transition. For now, we just want to be sure that the **Atomic** option is not flagged in the **Inspector** panel. The **Atomic** flag interrupts an animation, even if it has not finished playing yet. We don't want that to happen; when the character jumps, the animation must get to its end before playing any other clip.

The following screenshot hilights these options we just mentioned:

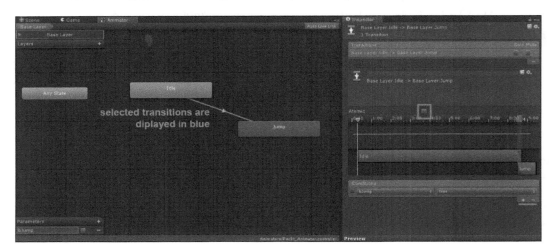

How it works...

We made our first transition with Mecanim and used a `boolean` variable called `bJump` to control it. It is now possible to link `bJump` to an event, for example, pressing the spacebar to trigger the **Jump** animation clip.

Coding the Boolean-based transitions

With the transition between **Idle** and **Jump** configured in the **Animator** window, we can script a piece of code to trigger it. With the following recipe, we show how simple it is to control animations through scripting with Unity.

Getting ready

As usual, we follow on from the last recipe. You just need to add a C# script in the `Scripts` folder of the project (as you learned in *Chapter 2*, *Importing 3D Graphics*) and name it `Char_Animator`.

How to do it...

1. Access the `Scripts` folder in your Project panel and double-click on the newly created script to open it in **Monodevelop**, the default Unity script editor.

2. Let's begin by creating an `Animator` type variable to store the reference to the character animator and add the following line at the top of the script:

    ```
    private Animator charAnimator;
    ```

3. Get inside the `Start()` function; here we need to address the `charAnimator` variable we created to the actual animator that we will attach to the character. We do that by adding the following line to the script:

    ```
    charAnimator=this.GetComponent<Animator>();
    ```

4. Now we define an event to trigger the `Jump` clip. In the `Update()` function, add the following lines to intercept the pressing of the bar and set `tJump`:

    ```
    if(Input.GetKey(KeyCode.Space)){
    charAnimator.SetBool ("bJump", true);
    }
    ```

Refer to the following screenshot to check whether your code is correct:

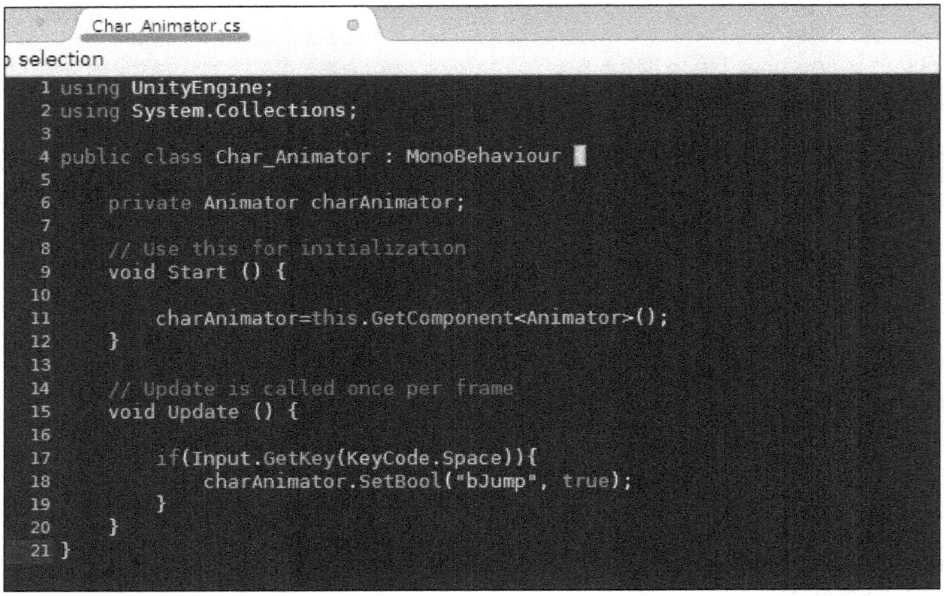

```csharp
1 using UnityEngine;
2 using System.Collections;
3
4 public class Char_Animator : MonoBehaviour
5
6     private Animator charAnimator;
7
8     // Use this for initialization
9     void Start () {
10
11         charAnimator=this.GetComponent<Animator>();
12     }
13
14     // Update is called once per frame
15     void Update () {
16
17         if(Input.GetKey(KeyCode.Space)){
18             charAnimator.SetBool("bJump", true);
19         }
20     }
21 }
```

5. Now, we need to add this script and the `Animator` controller to the character, but to do that, we first need to complete two steps:

    ❑   The first is to instantiate the character itself into the game scene, which we haven't done yet. Select **Character** in the project panel and drag it into the hierarchy or directly into the game scene. You can see this in the following screenshot. Also, be sure that translations and rotations from **Inspector** are all set to 0; it is strongly recommended!

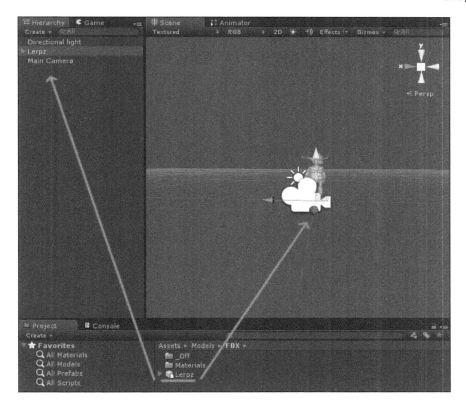

❑ The second step is to add the **Animator** component to the character in the scene. You can do that from the top menu or in **Inspector** (we go for the first solution). With **Character** selected in the scene, go to the menu and navigate to **Component | Miscellaneous | Animator**, as shown in the following screenshot:

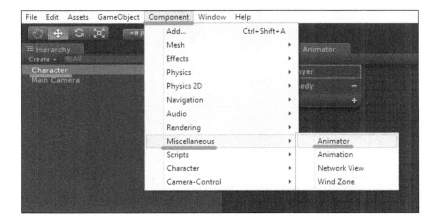

6. Now drag `Packt_Animator` from the `Animator` folder in the project panel in the `Controller` field of the **Animator** component into the **Inspector** window, which should display `None` in the Controller option field right now. Please refer to the following screenshot:

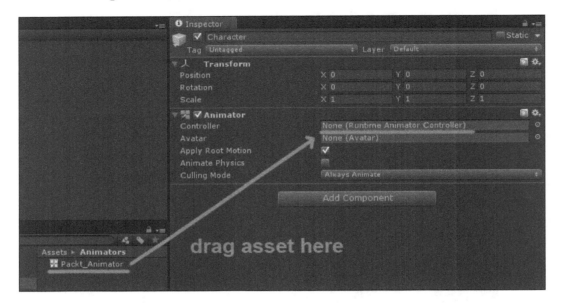

7. Next, drag `Char_Animator` from the `Scripts` folder onto the character in the scene. If you did things right, with the character selected, you should see both components displayed in the **Inspector** panel, as shown in the following screenshot:

8. Press the **Play** button to start your game scene in the editor. If you press the spacebar, the character jumps, playing the correct clip.

How it works...

Once transitions are set up, code is required to trigger them so that the animation clips are played. The logic to follow is pretty straightforward; we cover it here.

The character needs an animator component to store an animator controller. The controller holds the clips, represented as states; the transitions between them; and a number of control parameters to manage the logic. The script contains the instructions that trigger the clips in the animator controller, thanks to the control parameters.

All this information may seem overwhelming at first, but with practice, you'll see it makes perfect sense and you'll get used to it!

Working with float parameters

In the following recipe, we will show you how to use a `float` type to switch between clips based on a value that changes continuously, such as the character speed.

Let's assume we have an animation loop for the walking state of the character and another for running. As the character speed increases, it switches between the two states. How can we achieve that? Check out the following recipe to know.

Getting ready

As usual, we follow on from the previous recipe. Have the FBX files named `Char@Walk` and `Char@Run` imported and available in the project panel and the **Animator** window open in the editor.

How to do it...

1. Go to the **Project** panel and find the **Walk** and **Run** clips of your character. Drag them from the **Project** panel into the **Animator** window.
2. Right-click on the **Walk** animation and make a transition to **Run** and another back from **Run** to **Walk**.

3. Create a new parameter, this time a float variable, and name it fSpeed. The following screenshot shows the result you should have so far:

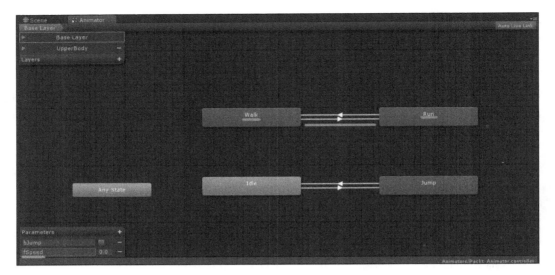

4. Click on the **transition** field to access its properties in the **Inspector** window.

5. Set fSpeed as the parameter to blend between **Walk** and **Jump**.

6. Once we set a float variable as the condition for the transition, we are also required to refine the condition itself by setting whether we want the transition to be performed once the value gets larger or smaller than a threshold we set. Set the threshold condition for our float parameter to **Greater** and set its value to 0.5. This way, the running clip is played as the character speed grows. Please refer to the following screenshot:

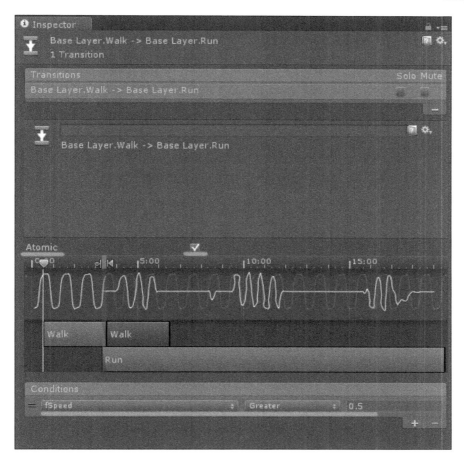

7. This time, we also flag the **Atomic** option, because we want this transition to be interrupted whenever the character meets the threshold we set.

How it works...

We added some complexity to the animation system of our character by adding a transition controlled by a `float` value. We used the `float` value to blend between the **Walk** and **Run** clips, based on the character speed. Assuming an analog control system, with this setup, the character switches between the **Walk** and **Run** clips based on the player's input.

Coding the float-based transitions

With this recipe, we show you how to use the actual speed of the character to update the value of a `float` variable. Once the values grow beyond the `0.5` threshold we defined in the **Animator** window, the **Run** clip is played.

Getting ready

Open the script named **Char_Animator** and be ready to edit the new lines we need to add the controls to switch between the walk and run clips.

How to do it...

1. First of all, we need to add a **Transform** variable to store a reference to the character in the scene:

   ```
   private Transform charRef;
   ```

2. In the `Start()` function, we initialize our **Transform** variable:

   ```
   charRef = this.GetComponent<Rigidbody>();
   ```

3. The `Rigidbody` function in the formula is a built-in component of Unity that allows physics to affect the game object. We will discuss this in a later chapter.

4. Next, we can add this single line in the `Update()` function of the script to make the `fSpeed` parameter equal to the character's horizontal speed, so that the proper animation clip is played depending on how fast the character is moving:

   ```
   charAnimator.SetFloat("fSpeed", charRef.rigidbody.velocity.z);
   ```

5. Next, we add another `if()` cycle to check whether the character is playing the **Idle2** animation, and in such a case, we reset the `fWait` parameter to `0.0`.

6. Please refer to the following screenshot, where the entire script is displayed, so you can be sure you coded it right:

```
Char_Animator.cs
Char_Animator  ▸  No selection
 1  using UnityEngine;
 2  using System.Collections;
 3
 4  public class Char_Animator : MonoBehaviour {
 5
 6      private Animator charAnimator;
 7      private Transform charRef;
 8
 9      // Use this for initialization
10      void Start () {
11
12          charAnimator= this.GetComponent<Animator>();
13          charRef = this.GetComponent<Rigidbody>();
14      }
15
16      // Update is called once per frame
17      void Update () {
18
19          if(Input.GetKey(KeyCode.Space)){
20              charAnimator.SetBool("bJump", true);
21          }
22
23          charAnimator.SetFloat("fSpeed", charRef.rigidbody.velocity.z);
24      }
25  }
```

How it works...

As you can see, coding the transition based on a `float` parameter was pretty easy, thanks to that `Rigidbody` component that stores the actual speed of a game object. We will discuss the **Rigidbody** component in detail in *Chapter 4, Taking Control*; what is important here is that we can equal the `float` parameter to the actual speed of the character to switch between clips.

There's more....

There is another relevant method available with **Animators** that is worth a mention, called `GetCurrentAnimatorStateInfo`.

This method takes an `int` parameter to specify the animator layer we are addressing to, which in our case is `0`, as we are only using one layer of animations for the character.

`GetCurrentAnimatorStateInfo` has a method of its own, called `IsName`, which allows you to check which animation clip is actually playing through a string parameter with the actual clip name.

The instruction would read like this:

`charAnimator.GetCurrentAnimatorStateInfo(int).IsName("string");`

Checking the actual state (animation clip) a game character is performing at any moment can be useful, for example, if you plan to chain clips together and allow the second to be triggered only if the first is already playing. Can you imagine a game situation where you would need this?

Creating Blend Tree

A very useful feature of the Mecanim system is the **Blend Tree**, which allows you to easily blend between two or more clips that can be controlled by a single `float` value. In fact, what if we plan to have our character switch between the idle, walk, and run states? With a **Blend Tree**, we can have the character's speed value take control of the conditions to switch between them, more or less as we did to switch between walking and running.

Follow us with the next recipe to learn how to use **Blend Trees**!

Getting ready

As we don't want to mess up the clips and transitions we created in the previous recipes, let's assume we are working with a clean animator controller. You can create a new one or clear the one we worked on before.

How to do it...

Access the Animator panel in Unity.

1. Right-click anywhere in the window (which should only contain the **Any State** box) and select **From New Blend Tree** under **Create State**, as shown in the following screenshot:

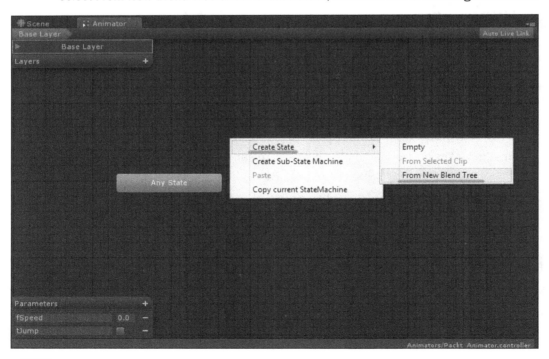

2. Double-click on the **Blend Tree** you just created to access its properties and configure it.

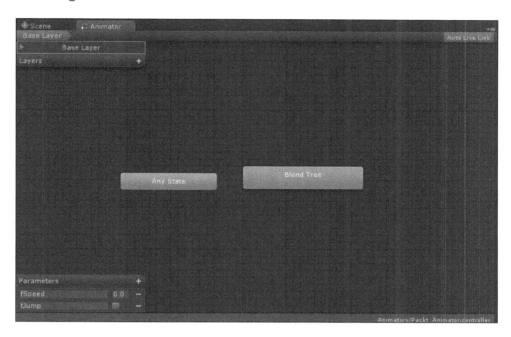

3. Move to **Inspector** and click on the small **+** icon in the **Motion** field. Then, select **Add Motion Field** from the menu, as shown in the following screenshot:

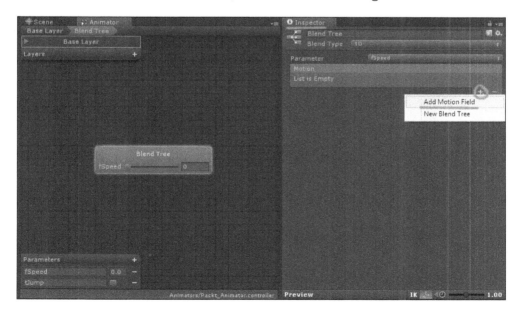

4. Do this two more times, then start dragging the animation clips from the project panel into the **Motion** fields we just created in the order shown in the following screenshot:

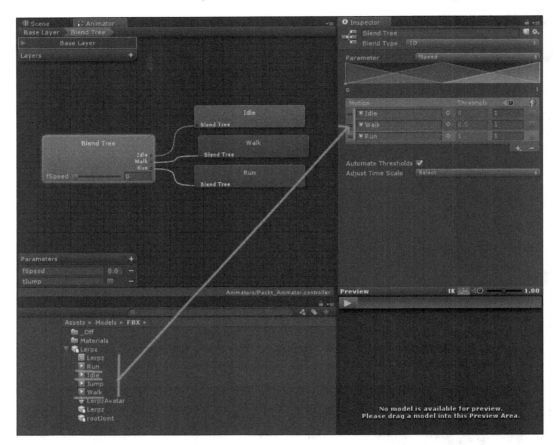

5. We now need to set the thresholds to decide at which speed the character stops being idle and goes walking, and from there to running. Click anywhere on the blue area representing the transitions to activate the **Threshold** fields and type in these values, as shown in the following screenshot: **0.2**, **0.5**, and **0.6**. The following screenshot shows the **Motion** section displayed in the **Inspector** window. Also, be sure that the fSpeed parameter we created before is selected from the **Parameter** drop-down menu!

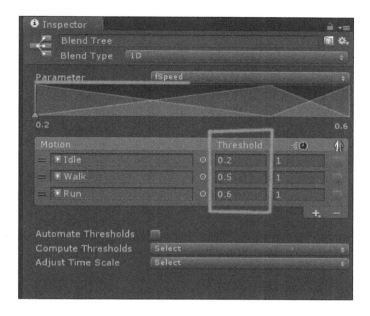

6. You can check the result in the **Preview** window by clicking on the small play button. If the **no model is available** message appears, simply drag the character model into the window.

How it works...

With the help of a **Blend Tree**, we now have a very efficient way to control the animations of the character with regard to its speed. By checking its value, we can smoothly switch between idle, walk, and run. And it only took a few steps to achieve it!

We suggest you experiment with this tool and maybe repeat this last lesson to get more acquainted with **Blend Trees**.

Animation layers – creating masks

With Mecanim, it is also possible to blend animations for different body parts of a character. Let's see an example. You have a character that runs with a gun in its hand and you have a reload animation that the character performs each time its weapon is empty. When the character reloads, you want his upper body, actually its arms, to perform the reload action, while the lower body of the character, its legs, should keep running.

To achieve that in Unity, Mecanim features what are known as layers. Layers allow you to create masks for specific body parts of a character and apply animation clips only on those parts. A running animation that involves legs and arms can be blended with a reload animation that only involves the character's arms, the result being that the character keeps running with its legs, while its arms reload the weapon!

As layers require masks to work, in the next recipe, we will show you how to make one.

Getting ready

As we are not prototyping a 3D shooter here, we are not going to use actual animation clips for this recipe. We only show the required steps to use layers, for the time you will be willing to use them.

Have your project open in Unity; we left it with the **Animator** control panel containing the animations we scripted so far: **Idle**, **Run**, **Walk**, and **Jump**.

How to do it...

1. If you take a look at the top-left corner of the **Animator** panel, you should see a box telling you we are working on **Base Layer**, as shown in the following screenshot:

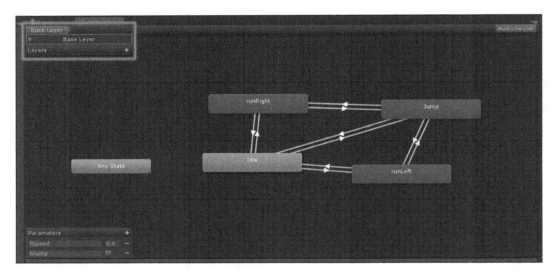

2. The first thing to do is create an `Avatar Mask` out of the character avatar we are already using. Let's begin by creating a new folder in the project and name it `Masks`. We have done this operation several times; you won't need a reference picture...

3. Now create a new `Avatar Mask` in this folder by right-clicking on the project panel and navigating to **Create | Avatar Mask**, as shown in the following screenshot:

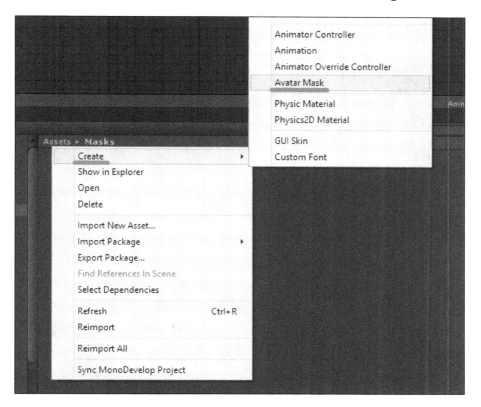

4. Name the mask `UpperBody`.

5. We now need to configure the mask by selecting the body parts that we want to be affected by our theoretical reload animation clip.

6. Select **UpperBody** in the project panel and move it to **Inspector**. You should see two menu buttons: **Humanoid** (this is because we set our avatar to **Humanoid** when we imported this character's animation clips in *Chapter 1, Importing 3D Models and Animations*) and **Transform**.

7. In the **Humanoid** panel, we have a representation of the character body. Right now, all body parts should be green, meaning that there is no selection made by the mask, yet. In this panel, green means that those parts are inside the mask and they will be affected by the layered animation clip, while red parts are out of the mask and the layered animation clip won't affect them. Clear enough?

8. Click on the head, body, legs, and shadow under the feet and the four small **IK** red dots to exclude them from the mask, as shown in the following screenshot. Basically, only the arms and hands must be green.

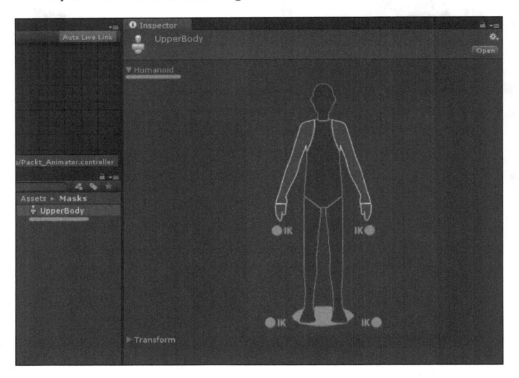

9. Now expand the **Transform** menu by clicking on it. You should have an empty field in the **Use skeletal from** parameter (displaying **None (Avatar)**!), meaning no reference avatar is available to create the mask, yet.

10. Click on the small button to the right to display the avatars available in your project and select one. At this point, you should have a **CharAvatar** available. Please refer to the following screenshot:

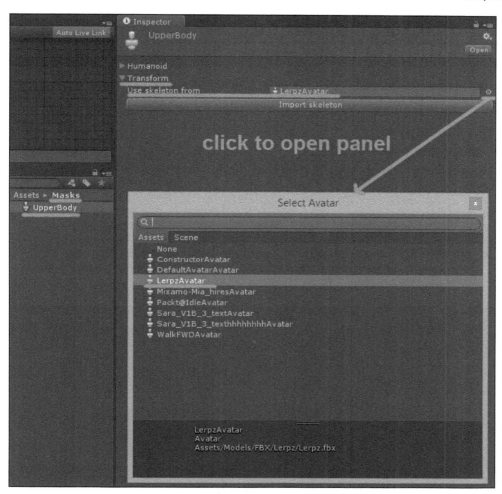

11. The mask is now saved and ready to be applied to a character.

How it works...

The principle to make masks is quite easy: starting from the actual avatar of your character, you can add or remove body parts to be included or excluded from those affected by specific animation clips. Thanks to Mecanim, the operation is quite transparent for the user! Still, many more settings are available that we didn't mention here, and we encourage you to refer to the manual, available at `http://docs.unity3d.com/Manual/class-AvatarBodyMask.html`.

Animation layers – adding a second animation layer

With the mask ready and set up, we can move back to the **Animator** panel to add a second animation layer. Be ready to follow our instructions.

Getting ready

We follow on from where we left off . The avatar mask is ready to be used with the second animation layer.

How to do it...

1. With the **Animator** editor open in Unity, click on the small **+** on the widget in the top-left corner of the window to add a new layer, as shown in the following screenshot:

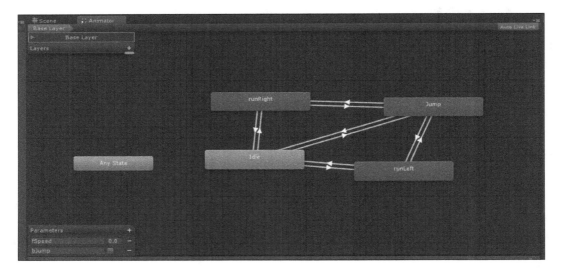

2. Click on the **Name** field and name this layer UpperBody, the same as the mask.
3. Set the **Weight** parameter to 1. This is sort of a default value; you may need to tweak it according to each of your actual animation clips.
4. Now click on the small button in the **Mask** field to select **Mask** from the panel, among the various options available in the project. Right now, you should see the **UpperBody** mask we created in the previous recipe. Please refer to the following screenshot for these last three steps:

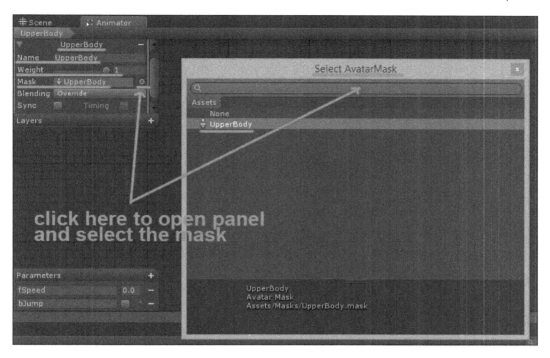

5. The last setting we are defining here is the blending mode we want for this **UpperBody** layer to work. If you click on the **Blending** drop-down menu, you can select two options: **Override** and **Additive**. In this case, we want **Override** to be set, because, thinking about the reloading while running case, we actually want the arms to reload instead of running.

6. **Additive** is fine, on the other hand, when you want the final animation to be the result of both clips mixed together. This is not what we want now. Please refer to the following screenshot:

7. Let's now focus our attention on the actual **Animator** panel. Right now, we don't have any state here, though we need two, at least: a default state, actually empty, and the reload animation clip (which we don't have for real!). Let's begin by adding an **Empty** state, as we did before. You can refer to the following screenshot and remember that this state must be colored orange, as it is the default state for this layer:

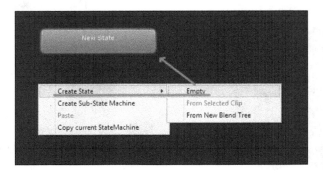

8. Now, assuming you actually have a reload animation to use, drag it from the project panel into the **Animator** editor, as shown in the following screenshot:

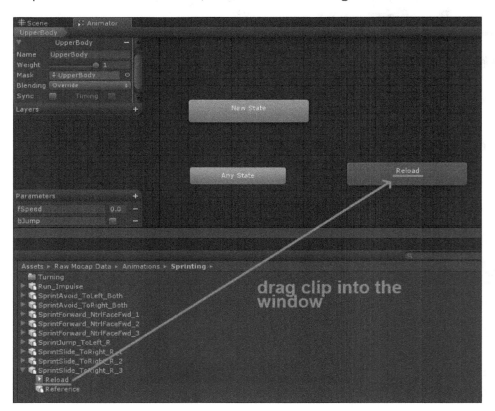

9. With the **Reload** clip added to the **UpperBody** animation layer, the next steps would be to create a new parameter, a `trigger`, or a `boolean` parameter like we used before; make a transition between the default state of **UpperBody** and reload; and finally, add instructions to the `AnimController` script to trigger the animation upon reloading the weapon.

10. Assuming you are going to use a `boolean` parameter called `bReload`, the line of code to be added would be:

```
charAnimator.SetBool ("bReload", true);
```

11. We won't repeat the steps here to perform these operations, as they follow the same logic we described in the previous recipe. Try to do this on your own this time!

How it works...

Mask blending and displacing animation clips on different layers is a technique that both allows you to create more complex animation trees for game characters while keeping the number of actual clips to be crafted at a minimum. In our case, we set a new layer to act only on the arms of the character and applied a reload animation clip to them, while the rest of the character's body keeps running, walking, or whatever.

As usual, we recommend you check out the manual for the more advanced settings, available at `http://docs.unity3d.com/Manual/AnimationLayers.html`.

There's more...

Mecanim is one of the most relevant improvements to Unity in recent years. There is really very much you can achieve with it, especially if you plan to use humanoid characters for full 3D games.

An option we didn't discuss in this chapter is retargeting, which allows you to adapt a complete animation set to different characters with similar skeletal configurations. Retargeting is an efficient and economic way, for example, to offer your players the option to choose between male or female characters to play with. Instead of making a complete new animation set for the additional characters, you just retarget the set you have!

We suggest you refer to the Unity documentation to learn more about the animator component, its features, and its methods. The manual is available at `http://docs.unity3d.com/Manual/AnimationSection.html`.

We suggest this tutorial (`http://www.digitaltutors.com/lesson/27480`) about character animation.

It is hosted by Digital Tutors: it is excellent, clear and quickly puts you on the track, though it comes with a price!

4
Taking Control

In this chapter, we will cover the following recipes:

- ▶ Creating a bumped material
- ▶ Importing packages
- ▶ Setting the Character Controller
- ▶ Adding Rigidbody
- ▶ Coding physics controls
- ▶ Collision management

Introduction

After we add an animation set for the character, we can finalize it before moving on to building an actual game level.

The character lacks a proper graphic aspect, game controls, and the capability to react to physics.

We are going to deal with these one at a time, starting with textures and materials. In *Chapter 2*, *2D Assets for Unity*, we described how simple materials are imported and created in Unity. Now that we have a true character for the prototype, we can discuss materials in more detail. In the following recipe, we create a material that requires two textures.

The material for the character we are working with requires two textures: one to provide the basic color of the mesh and another for the details of bumps and lights falling onto the mesh. The first texture or map is technically called the diffuse map of the character and, simply put, contains the information on how colors are distributed on the mesh surface without any lighting. The second is usually addressed as the normal map and it is the result of a computation to determine how light would strike the surface of the model, based on a very detailed version of that model commonly named high poly (meaning the model is made out of a large number of polygons). When creating video games, it is crucial to save as much memory as possible. Simulating the effect of lights on a mesh by using a map that applies the information obtained from a very detailed model to a low poly version of it is a commonly used technique to achieve such a result. This technique is called normal mapping.

Normal maps and texture mapping, in general, are two wide topics. For those of you who want to delve more into the matter, we suggest starting with these Wikipedia links: `http://en.wikipedia.org/wiki/Texture_mapping` and `http://en.wikipedia.org/wiki/Normal_mapping`.

Sorry for the parenthesis; it was necessary to at least introduce the subject before the recipe. Let's see how to create detailed materials to be applied to a game character.

Creating a bumped material

Technically speaking, we need to create a bumped diffuse material and use a diffuse texture and a normal map. The textures are provided along with this book, in the **Texture** folder of the package, so we just need to import them and use them for our detailed material.

Getting ready

In case you haven't done it yet, import the textures named `construcor_diffuse` and `constructor_normals` into the **Textures** folder of your Unity project.

How to do it...

1. Go to the **Project** panel in Unity and drag an instance of the constructor model into the scene. We modified it so it comes with a test checker texture attached to it.

2. In the **Materials** folder of your **Project**, create a new material by right-clicking on the folder and selecting **Material** under **Create** in the menu.

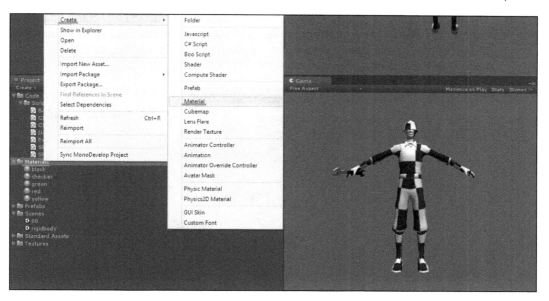

3. Name this material **mat_constructor**.

4. Select **mat_constructor** in the **Project** panel to access its properties in the **Inspector** window.

5. From the drop-down menu, change the **Shader** type from **Diffuse** to **Bumped Diffuse**, as shown in the following screenshot:

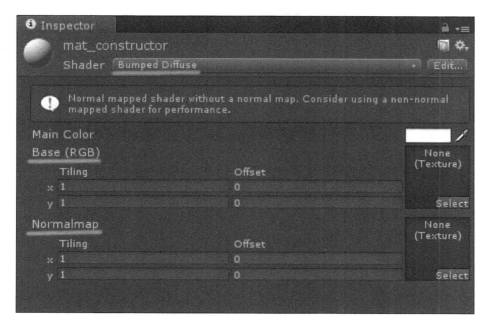

6. The **Bumped Diffuse** shader requires two textures, as we stated before: the diffuse map for the **Base** color and **Normalmap** for the lighting details. Click on the small **Select** button on the **Base Texture** slot and add the `constructor_diffuse` texture as the base map for the character.

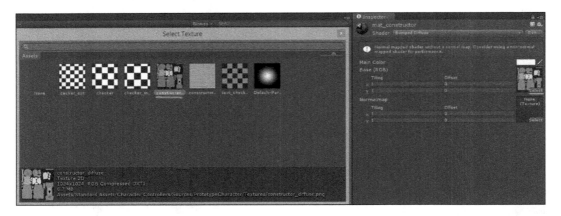

7. Now repeat the operation for the normal map slot and add the `constructor_normals` textures to provide the character with fine details.

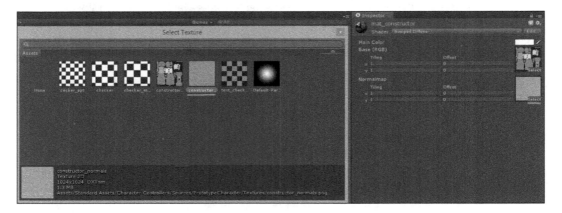

8. Drag the **mat_constructor** material onto the constructor model in the game scene to see the new material we just created. Be sure to also drag the material onto the wrench on the right-hand side of the model. The character finally looks like it is ready to be used in a game:

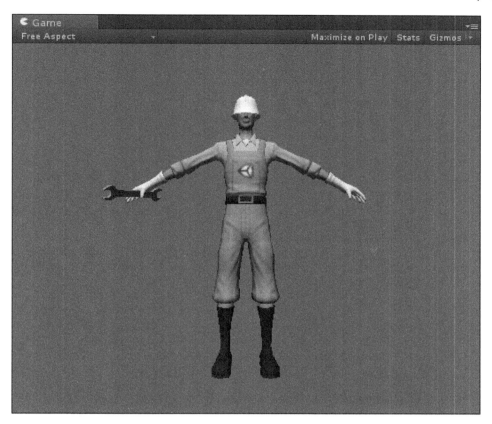

How it works...

A material can be intended as the result of the computation made by a (usually short) piece of code named a shader. The shader we used for this recipe, for example, takes two textures, the so called diffuse and normal maps. It then interpolates them according to an algorithm and finally produces the result we see on screen: a character model with a suit representing both the basic colors and the effect of light bouncing on its surface.

If you scroll through the shader options available in the **Material** panel of Unity Inspector, you can yourself check how many possibilities are available to create different types of materials for your game assets.

See also

Materials could cover an entire book of their own as it is a rich topic that deals with image crafting and programming at the same time.

Moreover, besides the built-in shaders available with Unity, new shaders can be added, bought, or programmed; the best hint we can give is to checkout the manual and forums if you want to delve deeper into materials. A good start is `http://docs.unity3d.com/Manual/Materials.html` and `http://docs.unity3d.com/Manual/class-Material.html`.

Taking control of the game character

With the materials added, we now need to subject the character to our will, implementing the game controls for our prototype.

When dealing with game controls in Unity, there are two approaches we can follow: we can use a Character Controller, which is a standard asset of Unity specifically implemented to control characters in first- and third-person perspectives, or we can rely on physics and take control of the character by applying forces to it with a Rigidbody, a built-in component of the Unity editor.

Character Controllers and Rigidbodies share a couple features that come in very handy when controlling a character, as they both provide collision detection and the means to move the character around. But this is where their similarities end—the two differ under all other aspects, especially with regard to movement, precision, and fluidity.

Character Controllers are excellent for shooters because they provide very responsive controls that don't take physics forces into much consideration, so to say. This is exactly what players require in games that mostly rely on reflexes! Think of any first-person shooter you have played; do you believe a real person could run all the time, strafe in the blink of an eye, or turn around so quickly?

On the other hand, Rigidbodies work fine, for example, for racing games that usually implement detailed physics models to simulate the actual behavior of vehicles in realistic environments. When you drive in a simulation game, you feel (or at least you should!) that the vehicle behavior is affected by acceleration, direction, vehicle setup, and maybe even the weather conditions, for the most advanced games.

Character Controllers and Rigidbodies are both valid choices with advantage points and drawbacks, so let's look at a couple of recipes to highlight the actual differences between them.

The important thing to stress upon is that one is designed for cases while the other is usually not. In other words, using a Rigidbody means you don't want to use a Character Controller, and vice versa!

Importing packages

The Character Controller package is a standard package provided with Unity and it can be added to a new project upon creating it, or it can be added in a later stage. As a starter, our next recipe shows how to import a package into an already existing project.

A large number of packages, such as the Character Controller package, are provided with Unity and more can be bought from the Asset Store. It's always worth taking a look to see what is available there whenever you need extra stuff for your projects. If you are lucky, you may find what you need for free. Otherwise, you can consider paying for quality stuff and save the time it would take to make it yourself.

Getting ready

Have your existing project opened in Unity and be ready to follow our instructions.

How to do it...

1. Access the **Project** panel and right-click anywhere. From the menu, select **Import Package** under **Character Controller**, as shown in the following screenshot:

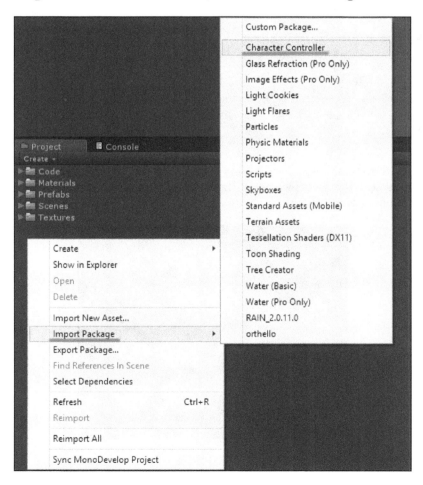

2. The importing panel opens. If you inspect it, you can see that the package is made of several components, including **Prefabs**, **Models**, **Textures**, **Scripts**, and so on. By flagging any of these components, you can decide what to actually import from a package and what not to import. In our case, we keep things easy and simply import everything contained in the package:

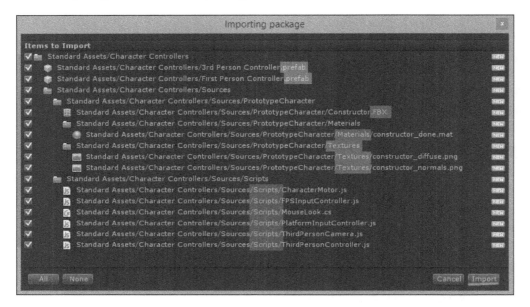

You should now have a new **Standard Assets** folder in the project, containing a **Character Controller** folder with the assets we need. The following screenshot displays what the project should now look like:

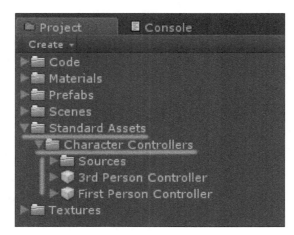

How it works...

The package is imported into the project and the **Character Controller** component can now be added to our game character. By inspecting the package in the **Project** panel, you can see that it contains several types of **Assets**, including **Prefabs**, **Textures**, and **Scripts**, as shown in the following screenshot:

The topic of our next recipe is to add **Character Controller** and set it up.

Setting the Character Controller

The Character Controller is designed for the first- and third-person control systems. It comes with movement control in all four directions, jump controls, and independent control of the camera, so the player can run in one direction and shoot in another.

A pretty clear way to describe the Character Controller is by saying that it is very precise with regard to movement, though it lacks fluidity: the character accelerates to maximum speed in the blink of an eye, turns on a dime, and stops the very moment you release the button. In other words, the feeling you get using a Character Controller is not very realistic, and to make it more fluid so it looks realistic, you need to turn to coding.

The Character Controller also doesn't implement physics by itself. It detects collisions but doesn't push or apply forces to the other GameObjects in the scene unless you program it to do so. As a matter of fact, it wouldn't even be affected by gravity if the scripts attached to it didn't make it!

As for collisions, the Character Controller only works with static Capsule Colliders. This means that it is specifically designed for things that resemble humanoid characters and that the Capsule Collider attached to the controller cannot be rotated when the mesh does.

On the other hand, the Character Controller has a pretty useful parameter called `isGrounded` that states whether a character has its feet on the ground. The variable is linked to another parameter called **Slope Limit** to set the maximum verticality of the surfaces we want the character to be able to climb on. Basically, it is a system that automatically prevents the character from walking on walls. Such a useful feature is not available with a Rigidbody.

Step Offset is another very useful parameter provided with Character Controllers that takes care of stating whether the character can step over an object or not. Thanks to this, we can allow the character to step over things such as steps or crates. With a Rigidbody, such elementary behavior must be specifically coded!

Many other properties are available to set up the Character Controller. With the next recipe, we show the most important ones, as we attach and set up a platforming-style Character Controller to our game character. Our plan is to prototype a side-scroller, and Unity offers exactly what we need. If you inspect the folder where we imported the **Character Controller** package, you should see a JS script named **PlatformInputController** in the **Scripts** folder. That's the script we are going to attach to the game character.

Getting ready

By dragging **PlatformInputController** onto the game character in the scene, four new elements appear in the **Inspector** panel: a component, the **Character Controller** itself, and two scripts—**CharacterMotor** and **PlatformInputController**. They are responsible for providing the character with the standard capabilities required by side-scrolling platform games, and by setting their properties, we define the behavior of our game character.

How to do it...

1. Access the Scripts folder in the **Project** panel. Select **PlatformInputController** in the `Scripts` folder of the **Character Controller** and drag it onto the game character in the scene.

2. The **Character Controller**, the **Character Motor**, and the **Platform Input Controller** components are added to our character. Now we can tweak their properties one by one to get the controls we like.

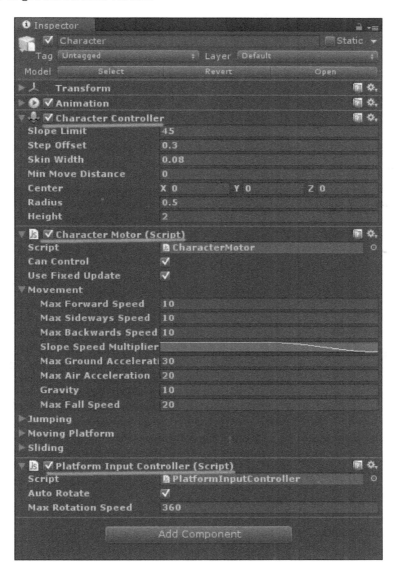

3. Let's begin by inspecting the **Character Controller** component. The **Slope Limit** parameter defines how steep the ground is so that the character is able to walk on it. Surfaces steeper than this value in degrees are considered walls and block the character. Very useful!

4. The **Step Offset** field defines the maximum height of objects that the character can step over. Unity manually suggests to keep this value between 0.1 and 0.4, assuming a standard character with a height of 2.0 in Unity units. And so we do!

5. The **Skin Width** field is a crucial parameter to prevent the character from getting stuck on walls and other obstacles should their respective colliders compenetrate each other. Very large values my cause the character to pierce into obstacles, while very small values may lead to no collision detection at all, so tweaking may become necessary with this parameter.

6. **Center**, **Radius**, and **Height** are pretty self-explanatory. **Center** defines the origin of the capsule collider that surrounds the mesh. **Radius** and **Height** are used to tweak the dimensions of the capsule to adapt it to the character model.

   Take a look at the following screenshot to check the configuration of the **Character Controller** component:

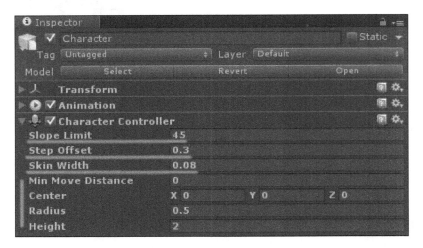

7. The **Character Motor** and **Platform Input Controller** scripts are predefined scripts that have been added with the package to the project. **Character Motor** defines the actual behavior of the character by controlling parameters such as its horizontal speed and acceleration, as well as jump height. **Platform Input Controller**, on the other hand, takes care of taking the input from the player and turning it into actual character actions on screen. We suggest you check out the forums to know more about these two important scripts. The following links are good ones to start with:

   ❑ http://forum.unity3d.com/threads/unity-3-character-motor-documentation.63917/

   ❑ http://answers.unity3d.com/questions/747207/side-scroller-controller-advice.html

How it works...

Adding **Character Controller** to a character basically means equipping the character with means to interact with the game world by defining its collider and how it walks on surfaces. Then, two scripts take care of the rest: **Character Motor** defines the behavior of the character, how fast it walks, accelerates, runs, or jumps, while **Platform Input Controller** takes care of turning the input from the player into character controls, specifically designed for platform games.

There is more...

By inspecting the properties of the **Character Motor** script, you may have noticed that a parameter called Gravity is available. You tweak this value to increase or decrease how strong the ground attracts the character when it falls.

We stated previously that the Character Controller doesn't implement gravity by itself, and that is still the case—while the Character Controller simulates physics through custom coding instructions of a script attached to the GameObject itself, gravity with the Rigidbody is based on the Unity physics engine, the renewed NVIDIA PhysX.

Adding Rigidbody

Another approach to control a game character is to use a **Rigidbody** component and make it subject to physics.

The Rigidbody adds several features to make a character behave as if it were a real physical object—it tends to fall down, it is pushed by other objects, and pushes them as well. If you want your game to have a realistic feel, then a Rigidbody is what you need.

The problem is that, more often than you may think, realism doesn't necessarily mean fun and engagement. As a matter of fact, the control style dependent on a Rigidbody is pretty realistic, but it is also not very precise. Momentum, friction, weight... these are all examples of variables you need to manage and appropriately tweak to get optimal game controls. In other words, with a Rigidbody you get fluidity, but you need to be comfortable with physics and have excellent programming skills to get true control.

With regard to gravity management, a Rigidbody has a parameter called **Mass** that defines how strong the character is attracted by the ground based on its physics properties. Imagine you have several GameObjects in your scene, each with its own Rigidbody. Should you decide to change the physics model as a consequence of a game event, you can change the defintion of gravity in your game and your changes will affect all Rigidbodies in the scene. With a Character Controller, you couldn't do that!

Another difference is that Rigidbodies allow us to use physics materials. A Rigidbody offers the opportunity to create special surfaces where the character slides as if it were ice, or slows down, or anything you may think of. This can be pretty useful for a platform game; however, the Character Controller doesn't support it!

With this recipe, we show you how you can add a **Rigidbody** component to a game character and how to tweak its parameters for a platform game.

Getting ready

Clean the game scene of any former character and add a new one. Follow the recipe to know what to do next.

How to do it...

1. Go to the **Project** panel and access the **Prefabs** folder. Now drag a new **Character prefab** into the scene and be sure it has no **Character Controller** attached to it.

2. With **Character** selected in the Hierarchy, click on the Component menu item and navigate to **Physics | Rigidbody** from the menu, as shown in the following screenshot:

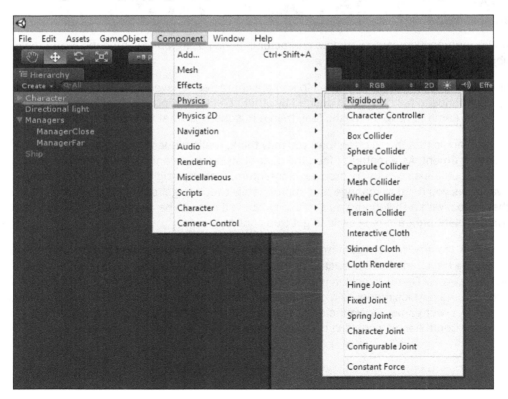

3. If you now move to the **Inspector** window, you can take a look at the parameters to control the behavior of the **Rigidbody**. **Mass** represents...well, the mass of a game object—how much it is subject to physics forces. Objects with high mass tend to fall down quickly, keep their momentum if they collide, and push other objects.

   An important thing to say about **Mass** is that it may happen that your imported models act strangely when added with a Rigidbody. The reason may be that the scale of your imported model is wrong. Always consider that in Unity, 1 unit = 1 meter, and that the physics engine works on the same exact scale.

4. **Drag** is another important parameter that defines the inertia of a game object. Low values of drag mean that the object is heavy, while high values mean it is light. Checking the manual, you may learn that 0.001 means a solid block of metal, while a value of 10 corresponds to a feather. Please refer to http://docs.unity3d. com/Manual/class-Rigidbody.html for an explanation of the **Drag** parameter.

5. **Is Kinematic** is an interesting option if you want a game object to detect collisions but don't want it to react to physics. For example, a classic 2D shooter requires collision detection but doesn't implement physics forces. Since an **Rigidbody** component may be necessary for detecting the collisions on a game object (check the collision detection tables at: http://docs.unity3d.com/Manual/CollidersOverview.html), the **Is Kinematic** option is a welcome feature of the **Rigidbody** component.

6. Finally, we have a set of properties called **Constraints**. By flagging these properties, we decide which axis the character can move to and rotate on. For example, for a side-scrolling game, you may want the character to not move on the *Z* axis, and freeze its rotations on the *X* and *Z* axes.

The following screenshot shows the settings to use a Rigidbody in our platform game:

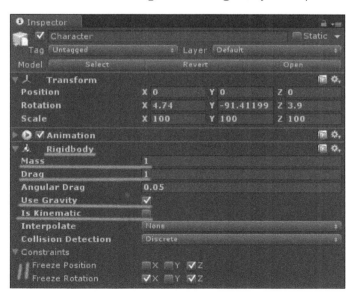

How it works...

A Rigidbody is one of those components you will keep making use of as you work with Unity. Game objects with Rigidbodies attached to them fall, push and can be pushed, have mass, provide a large collection of methods to interact with them, and can be fully controlled through physics. The settings we previously defined are those that meet the needs of our prototype; you may find yourself experimenting with them to find yours! With the **Rigidbody** component added to the character, we now have physics, but we still miss control. If we want to use physics forces interacting with the **Rigidbody** component to control the character, we need to script them. This is the topic of our next recipe.

Coding physics controls

In this recipe, we show you how to create a custom script to control a game object based on physics. It is not the final controller for the character of our prototype: it's a small piece of code that can be used for a classic 2D shooter, based on physics.

Getting ready

In the **Scripts** folder in the **Project** panel, create a new C# script and name it `PacktController`. Then, double-click on it to open it in **Monodevelop**.

How to do it...

1. First we need a bunch of variables to control the forces applied to the GameObject. Add the following lines at the beginning of the script, right below the usual line with the script class declaration:

```
(public class PacktController : MonoBehaviour {}):
public float horAcceleration;
  public float cruiseSpeed; //max speed when not pressing
  public float maxSpeed; //max speed while pressing
  public float actualSpeed; //speed at given time
  public float limY; //limit on y, use as mathf.abs
  public float expon; //used to smooth vert movement speed
  public float alpha; //use to tweak the vert movement
    speed
```

2. Now get into the `Start()` function and add the following line. We need to initialize `horAcceleration`:

```
horAcceleration = 4.0f;
```

3. Next we add a function to the script. Whenever you make use of physics, you should always put instructions into the `FixedUpdate()` function instead of `Update()`. The manual states that `FixedUpdate` should be used instead of `Update` when dealing with Rigidbodies. For example, when adding a force to a Rigidbody, you have to apply the force for every fixed frame inside `FixedUpdate()` instead of every frame inside `Update`. The reason is that `FixedUpdate()` is called at fixed time intervals and is not subjected to frame rate, thus providing better reliability with physics control.

4. These lines provide the actual speed of our character and set a parameter to smooth its movement:

```
actualSpeed = Rigidbody.velocity.x
expon = Time.time * alpha;
```

5. With regard to the x component of the `Rigidbody.velocity` vector we used, it assumes that the character model has been imported front-faced, as we learned in the first chapter of this book. Should you decide to do otherwise for any reason, just remember to take notice of that. With a character rotated 90 degrees on its *Y* axis, for example, the **z** component would affect speed, instead of the x component.

6. The following lines take care of controlling the left\right acceleration of the character by using the left and right arrow keys:

```
/* control left\right acceleration */
if (Input.GetKey (KeyCode.RightArrow) && Mathf.Abs (actualSpeed)
< maxSpeed)
    rigidbody.AddForce (Vector3.right * horAcceleration,
        ForceMode.VelocityChange);

if (Input.GetKey (KeyCode.LeftArrow) && Mathf.Abs (actualSpeed)
< maxSpeed)
    rigidbody.AddForce (Vector3.left * horAcceleration,
      ForceMode.VelocityChange);

if (Input.GetAxis ("Horizontal") != 0 && Mathf.Abs (actualSpeed)
> cruiseSpeed) {
    Vector3 v = rigidbody.velocity;
    v.x = (-v.x);
    rigidbody.AddForce (v, ForceMode.Acceleration);
}
```

7. Now we add the controls to have the game object fly up or down using the input coming from the Left and Right arrow keys. We also implemented a control to prevent the character from getting out of the top and bottom boundaries of the level:

```
//control up\down acceleration
  if (Input.GetKey (KeyCode.UpArrow)) {
    Vector3 v=rigidbody.velocity;
    v.y=(1-(Mathf.Exp(-expon)))*limY;
```

```
        rigidbody.AddForce(v,ForceMode.VelocityChange);
      }

    if (Input.GetKey (KeyCode.DownArrow)) {
      Vector3 v=rigidbody.velocity;
      v.y=(-1)*(1-(Mathf.Exp(-expon)))*limY;
      rigidbody.AddForce(v,ForceMode.VelocityChange);
    }
```

8. You can add the script to the character in the scene to apply this control system to it. The following screenshot shows the complete script:

How it works...

This script basically does two things. With regard to left\right acceleration, it provides a max speed that is reached while pressing the Left or Right arrow keys, whether the player is moving left or right. As the player releases the keys, the character slows down to a cruise speed, regardless of direction.

The script also prevents the character from going too far up or down. It sets a limit on the *Y* axis and then uses an asymptotic function to smooth down vertical speed upon reaching that limit.

You may have noticed that the function we are using to code our instructions is `FixedUpdate()`. When using **Rigidbody**, this is the function you must use, instead of `popularUpdate()`.

The other thing you should notice is that **Rigidbody** controls are coded as forces applied to the object as a consequence of the player input. In our case, we used the `Rigidbody.AddForce` method, which requires a vector to set the direction of the force applied to the R component (v) and the type of force applied (`ForceMode.VelocityChange`). We suggest you check out the manual for a thorough description of this method, available at `http://docs.unity3d.com/ScriptReference/Rigidbody.AddForce.html`.

Collision management

While describing the differences between Character Controller and Rigidbody, we have mentioned several times that both these components provide collision detection for the game objects they are attached to. Since collision detection is a fundamental task that must be performed by any game (at least, any game we can think of!) and it can be a hard dude to deal with, in the following recipe, we provide a few examples to show you how collisions actually work in Unity.

If you want to detect whether a collision happens between two game objects, you need both of them to be equipped with a Collider. A Collider is a sort of cage that contains the game object to check whether another game object enters its boundaries. When this happens, a collision message is sent to the system. Unfortunately, two colliders hitting each other won't generate a detection!

The minimal requirement for a collision detection in Unity is that one has both a Collider and a Rigidbody, and the other has at least the Collider. The Unity manual offers a table to show the minimal requirements for collision detection in Unity at `http://docs.unity3d.com/Manual/CollidersOverview.html`.

Getting ready

We use an entire new scene for our next recipe: create a new empty scene in your existing Unity project and be ready to follow our instructions!

How to do it...

1. Let's begin by creating a new **Scene** in the Unity project and adding a **Plane** game object to it.

2. Move **Plane** to the bottom of your game scene and resize it as you see fit so it acts as the floor for your scene.

3. Create a **Cube** and move it to the left and above the plane. You will notice that Unity automatically adds a **Box Collider** to it:

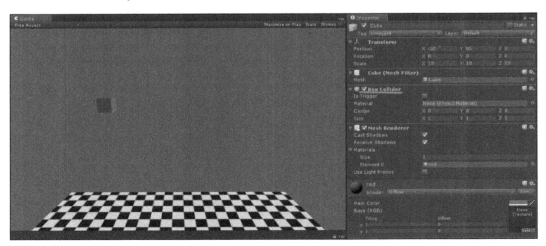

4. Add a Rigidbody component to the cube; we described how to achieve that in be specific.

5. Play your scene: the cube falls on the plane due to gravity and stops as it comes in contact with the plane because when we added the plane to the scene, Unity automatically added the Collider component to it, too.

6. To detect the collision, we need a script. Create a new C# script in the **Scripts** folder of the **Project** panel and name it `CollisionDetection`.

7. Double-click on the script to open it in **Monodevelop**.

8. Reach for the bottom of the script, outside the `Start` and `Update` functions, and add the following function:

```
void OnCollisionEnter(Collision collision)
{
   Debug.Log("Collision detected!");
}
```

9. Save the file, go back to Unity, and drag it from the **Project** panel to the **Cube** in the **Hierarchy** panel. The script should appear in the **Inspector** panel as a component of the **Cube**:

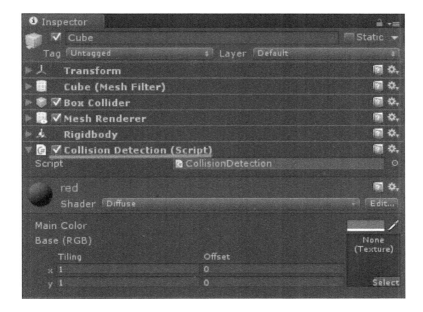

10. Run the application: as the cube touches the plane, the log message confirming that the collision has been detected is displayed.

11. Now add another GameObject to your scene, a sphere, and move it to the right side of the scene, with the same *y* and *z* coordinates as the cube.

12. Go back to the `CollisionDetection` script in `Monodevelop` and add the following line inside the `Update` function:

```
void FixedUpdate () {

    rigidbody.AddForce(8*Vector3.right,ForceMode.Acceleratio
      n);

}
```

With this line, we are instructing our cube to slowly move right on the *x* axis, towards the sphere we just added.

13. Go back to Unity, uncheck the **UseGravity** flag on the **Rigidbody** component of the **Cube**, and play the scene. The cube moves right and stops as it touches the sphere. The debug message is played as well.

How it works...

What happens is that the cube and the sphere collide, but upon collision, the cube stops, because the sphere has no physical properties, except in its physical existence as an obstacle in the path of the cube.

If we want the sphere to be influenced by the collision, a **Rigidbody** component must be added to the sphere, too. Do that and you'll see that when the cube hits the sphere, the latter will start moving as a consequence of the force it received from the collision!

There is more...

We don't fear repetitions: collision detection is a crucial component of games and it can be pretty harsh to deal with. Unity forums are exuberant with knowledge on the matter, so please refer to it whenever you have difficulties with collisions and the OnCollisionEnter() function in general at http://docs.unity3d.com/ScriptReference/Collider.OnCollisionEnter.html.

Also, remember that no solution is always good, so the best thing to do is to learn how to take advantage of the assets provided by Unity, depending on each specific condition.

We extensively discussed the differences between Character Controller and Rigidbody, so you can now decide which one better fits your needs. Finding the optimal balance between realism and fun is hard work and requires smart intuition. It is not by chance that this is one of the most important aspects in game design and balancing, which means that a lot of practice and experimentation are key to find that balance!

5
Building Up the Game Level

In this chapter, we will cover the following recipes:

- ▸ Creating Prefabs
- ▸ Coding a scrolling background
- ▸ Adding platforms
- ▸ Programming the character controls
- ▸ Setting up an Animator
- ▸ Adding collectibles to the game level
- ▸ Camera setup and controls

Let's get to work!

Introduction

With the character basically finished from a graphic standpoint, we can now start building up a game level for it to run around. This chapter is thus dedicated to creating an actual game level for our prototype and the logic to make it work as a side scrolling game.

Level design

Though we didn't discuss a design document for the prototype we are working on, with every new chapter we provided hints about the kind of game we plan to prototype. For those who didn't notice that, we will offer a recap here.

Our plan is to create a side scrolling running game. The character runs both left and right. There are platforms to jump on and collectible objects to gather. Gathering all collectibles means you beat the level, whereas falling from platforms more than a given number of times gets the player to the Game Over screen.

The camera displays the character from a side perspective and follows the character as it runs. Controls are standard and quite simple: left and right arrow buttons to move and the spacebar to jump.

The game has a background that procedurally recreates itself so the character can endlessly run in any direction: the background will always be there! Platforms are also created procedurally with criteria, so the character always has another platform close enough to jump on. The hard part with platforms is to create them so they are reachable by the character, based on its relative position.

Making the background for the prototype

We want the background elements for the game to be endlessly repeatable: for as far as the character can run in a direction, there will always be a piece of background behind it. To achieve that, we designed a background made of three panels: one stays in the middle and is centered on the player; the other two stay on the left and right of the central element. As the player runs, the farther element is replaced ahead of the character and this routine repeats as long as the game session goes on. The following screenshot shows what we mean:

The first thing we need is the actual panels; let's see how to make them.

Creating Prefabs

When you are working with Unity and need to instantiate a game object clone at runtime, you can take advantage of Prefabs. Prefabs are game object templates that can be configured however you like with regard to shape, material, behavior, and anything else you may need. These templates can then be saved in your project. Whenever you need that prefab in the game scene at runtime, you can use a function called `Instantiate()` that takes a prefab as a parameter and puts it in the game. The following recipe shows how to create Prefabs in Unity.

Getting ready

Start a new scene in your project and follow the instructions.

How to do it...

To make a prefab you first need to create a **GameObject**. Once you put everything you need into the GameObject, you can save it as a prefab.

1. Create a new **GameObject** in the scene, **Cube**. You should know by now how to do it.
2. Add the material called checker to **Cube** by dragging the material from the **Project** panel onto the object in the scene or into the **Material** slot in the **Hierarchy** (with the cube selected in the **Hierarchy**). You can refer to the following screenshot:

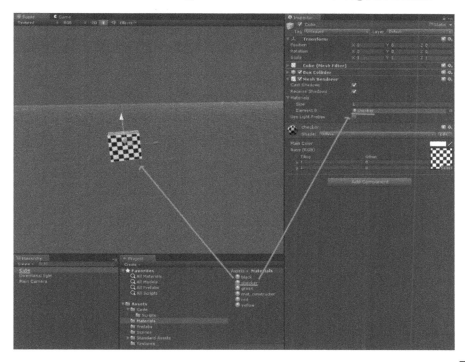

3. In the **Assets** folder of your project, create a new folder and name it `Prefabs`. Creating a folder is like creating any other type of asset: right-click on the **Assets** folder and from the menu, select **Folder** under **Create**.

4. Select the **Prefab** folder and right-click on it to create a new Prefab, as shown in the following screenshot:

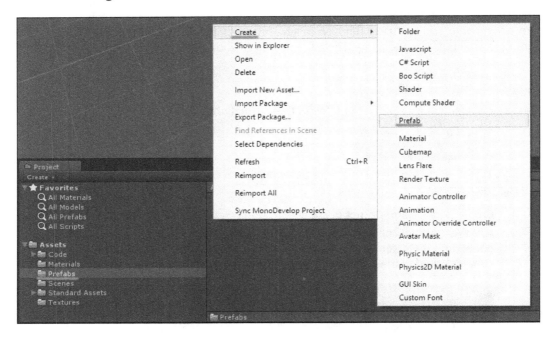

5. Name the **Prefab** `back_prefab`.

6. Check whether the cube in the scene is at the 0,0,0 position and with 0,0,0 rotation; then, drag it from **Hierarchy** into back_prefab in the **Project** panel, as shown in the following screenshot. If you did things right, the small square icon of back_prefab should turn from gray to light blue.

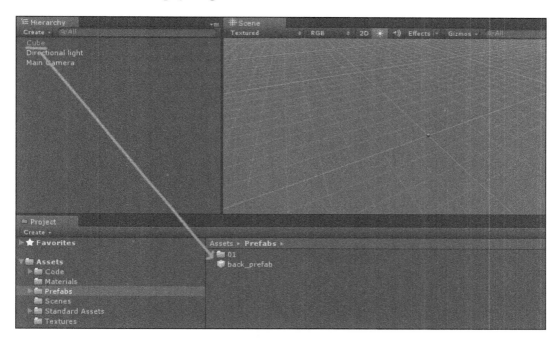

7. `back_prefab` is now ready to be instantiated at will in our game level. You can delete the cube from the scene, as we don't need it anymore and in the **Inspector**, check whether `back_prefab` is actually a cube with a checkered material, as shown in the following screenshot:

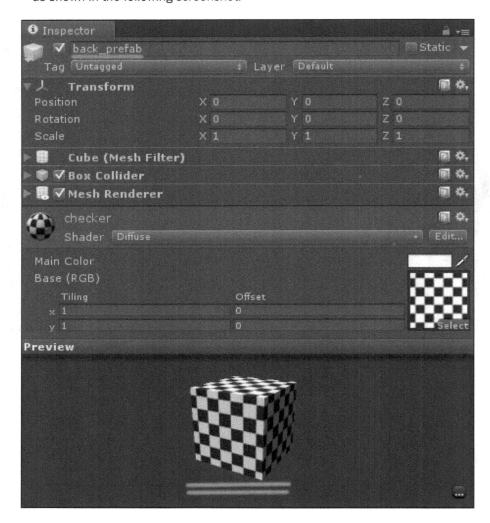

How it works...

The procedure to make prefabs is always the same, regardless of the actual characteristics of the game asset itself: create a game object in the scene, add anything you want/need/like to it to define its graphic aspect and behavior, then drag the game object onto a prefab and delete the game object from the scene. Voilà!

The prefab to be used for the background is ready, so we now need to script its behavior to use it for the prototype. This is what we will do in the next recipe.

Coding a scrolling background

We will keep going with the same game scene we left at the end of the previous recipe, so just stick with the instructions!

How to do it...

1. In the **Scripts** folder of your **Project** panel create a new C# script and name it `Back_Manager`.

2. Double-click on the script to open it in **Monodevelop**.

3. Let's begin by creating the required variables: we need one public Transform variable to store the reference to the prefab to be used as the background panels and a few private vars to define things like the scale of the panels, the distance from the character, and a reference to the game character.

    From a game logic perspective, the most important variable we are adding to the script is an `Array[]` variable type that we use to manage the three panels that repeat endlessly in the background. To achieve that, add the following lines at the beginning of the script:

    ```
    public Transform backBrick;

    private Transform[] backArray=new Transform[3];
    private Transform thisChar;
    private float distance;
    private float farDistance;
    private Vector3 brickScale;
    ```

4. In the `Start()` function we put the instructions to initialize the variables and create a service `float` variable to help us make longer lines of code more readable. These instructions could be added to an `Awake()` function instead of `Start()`, but to keep things easy, we prefer to use the `Start()` function.

5. Add the following lines to the `Start()` function of the script:

    ```
    thisChar = GameObject.Find ("Constructor").
    GetComponent<Transform>();
    farDistance = 30.0f;
    brickScale=new Vector3(60,60,1);
    float xPosition;
    ```

6. Now we add a `for()` cycle to instantiate the panels in the scene; add them to the array and set their scale. The following code goes into the `Start()` function too:

```
for (int i=0; i<3; i++) {

  xPosition=(brickScale.x*i);
  backArray[i]=(Transform)Instantiate(backBrick,new Vector3
    (xPosition,0,farDistance),Quaternion.identity);
  backArray[i].localScale=brickScale;
}
```

7. In the `Update()` function we plan to run a routine that keeps repeating and checks the horizontal distance between the character and the background panels. For this reason, instead of coding the routine into the `Update()` function itself, we make a custom function and then call that function in `Update()`. The custom function name is `CheckDistance()` and this is the code to be added to it:

```
void CheckDistance(){

  for (int i=0; i<3; i++) {

    distance=thisChar.transform.position.x
           backArray[i].transform.position.x;

    if(Mathf.Abs (distance) > (brickScale.x * 1.5) &&
          distance > 0){
      backArray[i].Translate( 3* brickScale.x,0,0);
      break;
    }

    if(Mathf.Abs (distance) > (brickScale.x * 1.5) &&
          distance < 0){
      backArray[i].Translate(-3*brickScale.x,0,0);
      break;
    }
  }
}
```

8. Access the `Update()` function and add a call to `CheckDistance()` there using the following lines:

```
void Update () {
  CheckDistance ();
}
```

In case you are missing something, the following screenshot shows the complete `BackgroundManager` script:

```
1  using UnityEngine;
2  using System.Collections.Generic;
3
4  public class BackgroundManager : MonoBehaviour {
5
6      public Transform backBrick; //prefab to be used for background
7
8      private Transform[] backArray=new Transform[3]; //array used to store background panels
9      private Transform thisChar; //used to store the reference to the ship for distance check
10     private float distance; //used to check distance between ship and bricks
11     private float farDistance;
12     private Vector3 brickScale; //scale for bricks
13
14     void Start(){
15
16         thisChar = GameObject.Find ("Constructor").GetComponent<Transform>();
17         farDistance = 30.0f;
18         brickScale=new Vector3(60,60,1);
19
20         float xPosition; //used to store the sum-subtraction-multiplication to make instantiate more readable
21
22         for (int i=0; i<3; i++) {
23             xPosition=(brickScale.x*i);
24             backArray[i]=(Transform)Instantiate(backBrick,new Vector3 (xPosition,0,farDistance),Quaternion.identity); //instantiate the bricks
25             backArray[i].localScale=brickScale; //set bricks scale
26         }
27     }
28
29     // Update is called once per frame
30     void Update () {
31
32         CheckDistance (); //I use a function inside Update() to avoid using a for inside update.
33     }
34
35     void CheckDistance(){
36
37         for (int i=0; i<3; i++) {
38             distance=thisChar.transform.position.x-backArray[i].transform.position.x;
39
40             if(Mathf.Abs (distance) > (brickScale.x * 1.5) && distance > 0){ //check that a new brick needs to be inst. L/R
41                 backArray[i].Translate( 3* brickScale.x,0,0); //I multiply by 3 because we are using 3 bricks for the background
42                 break;
43             }
44             if(Mathf.Abs (distance) > (brickScale.x * 1.5) && distance < 0){
45                 backArray[i].Translate(-3*brickScale.x,0,0);
46                 break;
47             }
48         }
49     }
50 }
```

9. Go back to Unity, create an empty **GameObject** in the scene and name it `back_manager`. You can refer to the following screenshot:

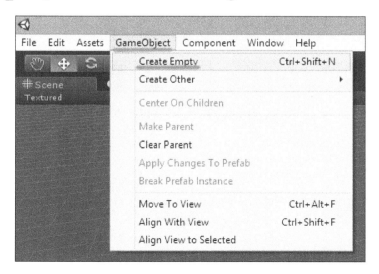

10. Now drag **Back_Manager** onto the **back_manager** game object in the scene. The attached script, called Back Brick, should appear in **Inspector** as it's one public variable.

11. Drag **back_prefab** from the **Project** panel onto the **Back Brick** slot of the **BackgroundManager** script in the **Inspector**, as shown in the following screenshot:

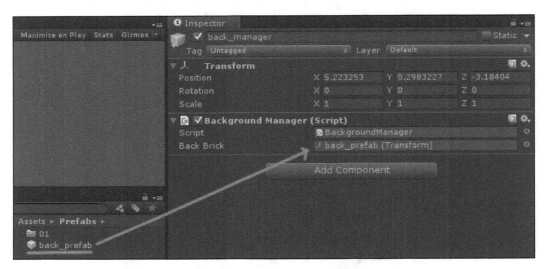

How it works...

The scripts attached to `back_manager` in the scene take care of instantiating the panels with the right position and scale. As the character moves left or right, the scripts check their position and decide how to translate the background panels so one is always behind the player. It just needs us to manually create a reference to the prefab to be used for the background panels, which is what we did with the last step of the recipe.

Adding platforms

We can now move on to building and coding the platforms we need for the character to jump on. In this prototype, we want platforms to be created according to the character's direction, left or right. This is consistent with the idea of building a two-way side-scrolling game. We also want to add a bit of variety so we code platforms of random length and with random vertical and horizontal gaps between them as well.

As for the elements we used for the background, we need a prefab and a piece of code.

Getting ready

Let's begin by making the Prefab. Follow the same steps described in the first recipe of this chapter to make a prefab called `plat_prefab` and add a material of your choice to it. You know how to do it.

For your reference, we have added a screenshot here to show you what a platform in the scene should look like:

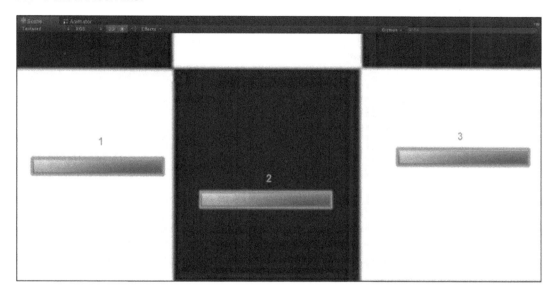

Next, we can write the script.

How to do it...

1. In the `Scripts` folder of your project, create a new C# script and name it `PlatManager`; then open it in **Monodevelop**.

2. As usual, we declare the public and private variables at the top of the script. This time we need plenty: transforms for the character and the platforms to be instantiated in the scene and several float values and vectors to define positions and gaps. Add the following lines to **PlatManager**:

```
public Transform platBrick;
private Transform thisChar;
private Transform actualPlat, prevPlat, nextPlat;
private Vector3 platScale;
private Vector3 nextPos;
private float charX, charY, charZ;
private float gap, delta, yGap;
private float maxY, minY;
```

3. In the `Start()` function we initialize the variable storing the reference to the character, use `float` to handle level boundaries and intervals, and create the first platform right below the character spawning point. Add the following lines to the script. The `SetScalesAndGaps()` function is defined at the bottom of the script:

```
void Start(){

    thisChar =
                    GameObject.Find("runner").
    GetComponent<Transform>();
      maxY = 30f;
      minY = -10f;
      delta = 4; //we use this to define intervals
      nextPos = new Vector3(charX, charY - 1.5f, charZ);
      actualPlat = (Transform)Instantiate(platBrick, nextPos,
        Quaternion.identity );
      SetScalesAndGaps();
      actualPlat.localScale = platScale;
      prevPlat = null;
      nextPlat = null;
}
```

4. The `SetScalesAndGaps()` function is meant to generate all random values we need to scale the platforms and set horizontal and vertical gaps between them. We decided to put all the instructions in a single function so the script is more compact. The `CheckYGap()` is a small function to check that the `yGap` random generated value lies between the top and bottom limits we defined for our game level:

```
void SetScalesAndGaps(){
    platScale = new Vector3(Random.Range(20,28),1,1);
    gap = Random.Range(8f,16f);
    if(prevPlat != null){
      yGap = prevPlat.transform.position.y + (Random.Range (
          delta,delta));
      CheckYGap();
    }
}
```

5. What follows is the code for the `CheckYGap()` function, which takes advantage of the `minY` and `maxY` variables we set before:

```
void CheckYGap(){ //we set top and bottom vertical limits
    if (yGap > maxY){
      yGap = maxY;
    }
    if(yGap < minY){
      yGap = minY;
    }
}
```

6. There is a last function we created to update the actual character position. It is called `UpdateCharPos()` and these are the lines to put into it:

```
void UpdateCharPos(){ //update char pos
  charX = thisChar.transform.position.x;
  charY = thisChar.transform.position.y;
  charZ = thisChar.transformposition.z;
}
```

7. Now we can address the `FixedUpdate()` function of the script. As you may remember, the `FixedUpdate()` function should be used instead of `Update()` whenever you want to use Rigidbodies and physics in the scene. In our case, we first update the character position, then we check whether it is going left or right. That done, we define the scales and gaps, calculate the next position and finally instantiate a platform using the prefab we made earlier. Add the following code to the `FixedUpdate()` function:

```
UpdateCharPos();

if(actualPlat != null && charX > actualPlat.transform.position.x +
delta){
  float strict = actualPlat.transform.position.x;
  prevPlat = actualPlat;
  actualPlat = null;
  SetScalesAndGaps();
  nextPos = new Vector3(strict + platScale.x + gap, yGap,
      charZ);
  nextPlat = (Transform)Instantiate(platBrick, nextPos,
      Quaternion.identity );
  nextPlat.localScale = platScale;
}

if(actualPlat != null && charX < actualPlat.transform.position.x -
delta){
  float strict = actualPlat.transform.position.x;
  prevPlat = actualPlat;
  actualPlat = null;
  SetScalesAndGaps();
  nextPos = new Vector3(strict - platScale.x - gap, yGap,
    charZ);
  nextPlat = (Transform)Instantiate(platBrick, nextPos,
      Quaternion.identity );
  nextPlat.localScale = platScale;
}
```

8. Next we check whether the character has reached the next platform, or if it, instead, inverted its direction using a couple of `if()` statements:

```
if(prevPlat != null){
   float strict = prevPlat.transform.position.x;
   if(charX > strict - delta && charX < strict + delta){
     Destroy(nextPlat.gameObject);
     nextPlat = null;
     actualPlat = prevPlat;
     prevPlat = null;
   }
}

if(nextPlat != null){
   float strict = nextPlat.transform.position.x;
   if(charX > strict - delta && charX < strict + delta){
     actualPlat = nextPlat;
     nextPlat = null;
     Destroy(prevPlat.gameObject);
   }
}
```

9. The coding for this recipe ends here. The next step is to drag the script from the `Project` folder onto a game object in the scene. As we did for **back_manager**, add an empty **GameObject** to the scene, name it `platform_manager`, and drag the `PlatManager` script onto it.

10. Now drag the **plat_prefab** asset in the **Prefabs** folder of the project into the `platBrick` variable slot of **platform_manager** in the **Inspector** panel. These are the exact same steps we performed for the previous recipe.

How it works...

In this implementation, platforms are created depending on the direction of the character, once it gets beyond the center of the platform it is actually on, at any moment.

The script also considers the possibility that the player changes their mind and inverts the direction the character is running in. In such a case, the last platform created is destroyed and the cycle repeats.

We encourage you to experiment with alternative methods to control platforms and improve our prototype system. For example, you may want the platforms to disappear after a short time interval so the player is forced to keep running.

Also, you can use an entirely different method to manage platforms: there's this technique called **object pooling** that is actually more efficient, as it doesn't require you to destroy and create platforms every time. The following links are a good starting point to learn this methodology:

- ▶ `http://gamedevelopment.tutsplus.com/tutorials/object-pools-help-you-reduce-lag-in-resource-intensive-games--gamedev-651`
- ▶ `http://gameprogrammingpatterns.com/object-pool.html`

There's more...

Another interesting thing you could do to improve the gameplay of this prototype is to take advantage of so-called physics materials to create platforms that affect the responsiveness of the character controls, for example, slowing it down or making it slide like it's running on ice. We suggest you take a look at the following link: `file:///C:/Program%20Files%20(x86)/Unity/Editor/Data/Documentation/Documentation/Components/class-PhysicMaterial.html`.

Programming the character controls

Though we already mentioned a few examples of game controls with Rigidbody and Character Controller, in the following recipe, we will code the actual controls for the game character of our prototype. We couldn't do this before we had working platforms in the prototype! In the following recipe, we will make use of the Rigidbody component and its physics features, plus add in a few simple instructions.

Getting ready

Open up your project. We need a new script for this, so create one as usual in the `Scripts` folder of your project and name it `Runner`.

How to do it...

1. As usual, the script begins with the variable declarations. We need a reference to the Animator attached to the character for the animations, variables for horizontal and vertical acceleration, and a Boolean variable to take notice whether the character is touching the ground, among the others.

    Add the following lines at the bottom of the script:

    ```
    public static float distTraveled;
    public static bool bIsTouch;
    private float horAcceleration;
    private Animator charAnimator;
    private Vector3 jumpVel;
    private Transform nextPlat;
    ```

2. In the `Start()` function, we initialize the variables we need at the beginning of the script with the following lines:

    ```
    void Start () {
      charAnimator =
                        GameObject.Find("runner").
    GetComponent<Animator>();
      horAcceleration = 4f;
      bIsTouch = false;
      jumpVel = new Vector3 (0,10,0);
    }
    ```

3. In the `Update()` function, we control the speed of the character so that it stays below an arbitrary value that fits our gameplay and also takes into account of the distance traveled by the character, as it may be useful later. Since we are using a Rigidbody component, the relevant code for character controls goes into the `FixedUpdate()` function.

    Add the following lines into the `Update()` function:

    ```
    void Update () {

      if (rigidbody.velocity.x > 6f){
        Vector3 v = new Vector3(6f, 0, 0);
        rigidbody.velocity=v;
      }
      if (rigidbody.velocity.x < -6f){
        Vector3 v = new Vector3(-6f, 0, 0);
        rigidbody.velocity=v;
      }

      distTraveled=transform.localPosition.x;
    }
    ```

4. Before getting to `FixedUpdate()`, let's take a look at the `OnCollisionEnter()` and `OnCollisionExit()` functions that we use to set `bIsTouch` to control whether the character is actually touching a platform. We also set a variable on the Animator to trigger the jump animation clip. Add the following lines to the script:

```
void OnCollisionEnter(Collision c){

  if(c.gameObject.tag == "platform"){
    bIsTouch = true;
    charAnimator.SetBool("bJump",false);
  }
}

void OnCollisionExit(Collision c){
  Debug.Log(bIsTouch);

  if(c.gameObject.tag == "platform"){
    bIsTouch = false;
    charAnimator.SetBool("bJump",true);
  }
}
```

5. To get these functions to work, we need to define a tag and assign it to the platform triggering the collision, referenced to as `Collision c` in the script. To do that, select **plat_prefab** in the **Project** panel, then move to **Inspector**, and click on the drop-down menu in the Tag field. Select **Add Tag...** from the menu, as shown in the following screenshot:

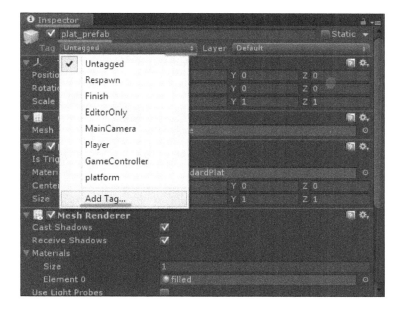

6. Set **Size** to 2 and name the first empty field `platform`, as shown in the following screenshot:

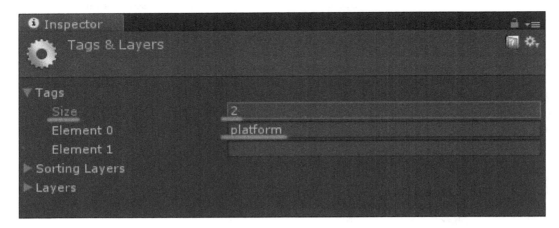

7. Now select **plat_prefab** again in the **Project** panel and, from the **Tag** menu in **Inspector**, select the **platform** tag that should now be available. You can refer to the following screenshot:

8. Back to the script now. In the `FixedUpdate()` function, we take the player input (left or right) and use it to add a horizontal speed to the character. We also use the horizontal speed of the character to trigger the running animation.

   Add the following lines into the `FixedUpdate()` function:

```
rigidbody.velocity = new Vector3 (Input.GetAxis("Horizontal") *
horAcceleration,
    rigidbody.velocity.y, rigidbody.velocity.z);
charAnimator.SetFloat("fSpeed",rigidbody.velocity.x);
```

9. Next we control the horizontal speed of the character to switch between the left or right running animation with these lines:

```
if(rigidbody.velocity.x > 0f){
    Quaternion rot = Quaternion.Euler(new Vector3(0,90,0));
    rigidbody.rotation = rot;
}
if(rigidbody.velocity.x < 0f){
    Quaternion rot = Quaternion.Euler(new Vector3(0,-90,0));
    rigidbody.rotation = rot;
}
```

10. Finally, we allow the player to use the spacebar to make the character jump. In doing so, we check whether the character is actually touching the ground; we then add the `jumpVel` vector to the character velocity and set `bIsTouch` to `false`. Add the following lines at the end of `FixedUpdate()`:

```
if(bIsTouch == true && Input.GetKeyDown(KeyCode.Space)){
    rigidbody.AddForce(jumpVel,ForceMode.VelocityChange);
    bIsTouch=false;
}
```

11. The following screenshot shows the complete `FixedUpdate()` function of the script:

```
57
58  void FixedUpdate(){
59
60      rigidbody.velocity = new Vector3 (Input.GetAxis("Horizontal") * horAcceleration, rigidbody.velocity.y, rigidbody.velocity.z);
61      charAnimator.SetFloat("fSpeed",rigidbody.velocity.x);
62
63      if(rigidbody.velocity.x > 0f){
64          Quaternion rot = Quaternion.Euler(new Vector3(0,90,0));
65          rigidbody.rotation = rot;
66      }
67      if(rigidbody.velocity.x < 0f){
68          Quaternion rot = Quaternion.Euler(new Vector3(0,-90,0));
69          rigidbody.rotation = rot;
70      }
71
72      if(bIsTouch == true && Input.GetKeyDown(KeyCode.Space)){
73          rigidbody.AddForce(jumpVel,ForceMode.VelocityChange);
74          bIsTouch=false;
75      }
76  }
```

How it works...

What we implemented is a fairly basic control system based on physics. We add a force to the character when the player hits the left or right button and we prevent the speed from getting too high. We also check whether the character is actually touching the ground before allowing jumps, and whether it prevents the player from jumping while in midair.

When you apply a force to a Rigidbody with the `Rigidbody.AddForce()` method, there are several options available with regards to the type of force applied. In this case, we use the `VelocityChange` type, which determines an instant change of force, which is useful for our prototype to have the character instantly change the direction it is running in. Other options are available: we suggest you check the manual available at `http://docs.unity3d.com/ScriptReference/ForceMode.html`.

There's more...

This control system needs many refinements. Still we think we got to the point of how to approach the problems related to side-scrolling with physics. You can move on and refine it yourself. What about providing the character with a max speed parameter and adjusting the jump distance to that value?

When we approached the character Animator for the first time, we provided examples on how to take advantage of its features. Now that we have a fully animated character, we can fine-tune the Animator to trigger the animation clips we need, when we need them. This is the topic of our next recipe!

Setting up an Animator

Double-click on `Packt_Animator` from the **Project** panel to open the **Animator** panel in Unity. If you messed up a little with it, delete anything except the default **Idle** node.

How to do it...

1. Create three new empty states by right-clicking anywhere in the **Animator** window, then select **Create State** and **Empty**, as shown in the following screenshot. Name them **runRight**, **runLeft**, **Idle** and **Jump**.

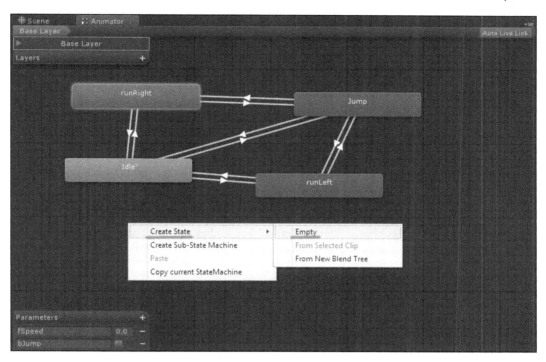

2. Add the run animation clip to both **runRight** and **runLeft** states, as shown in the following screenshot:

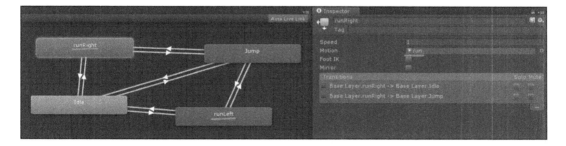

3. Lastly, add the **jump_pose** clip to the **Jump** state. Here's a screenshot, just in case:

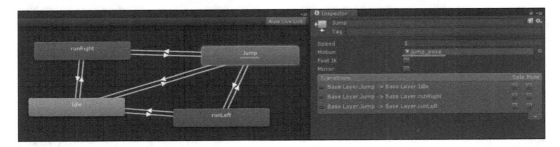

4. Now we can take care of the transitions. First of all we need two variables: a float called **fSpeed** to check whether we should trigger the left or the right sided running animation, and a Boolean called **bJump** for jumping. You should remember how to do this. The following screenshot shows what you are searching for:

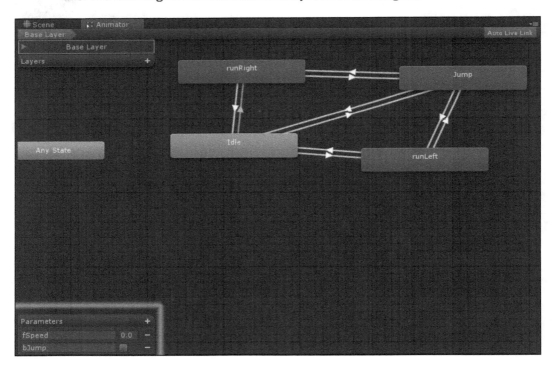

5. Create a new transition from **Idle** to **runRight**, and in the **Inspector** panel, set the condition to **fSpeed** greater than 0.2, as shown in the following screenshot:

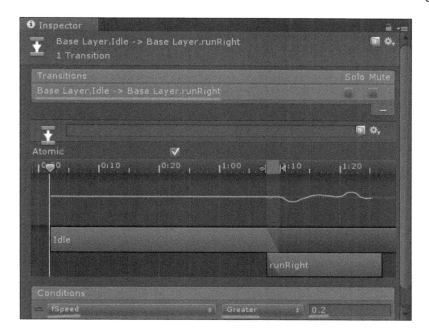

6. We also need to create a transition back from **runRight** to **Idle** and set the condition for triggering the transition as follows: we trigger the animation when the **fSpeed** parameter has a value below 0.2. Check the following screenshot to be sure you are doing things right:

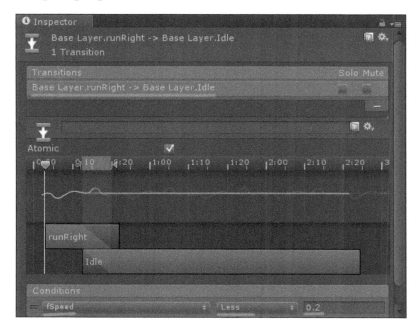

7. Repeat the same operation with **Idle** and **runLeft**, but this time the enter condition is that **fSpeed** is less than -0.2, while the exit condition is that **fSpeed** is greater than -0.2.

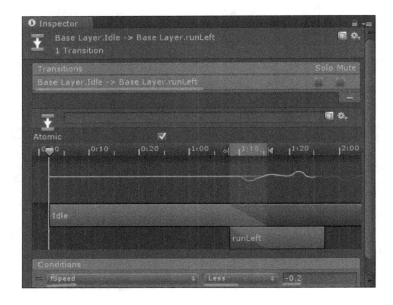

The reason for this is that when the character runs left, it is going towards negative values on the *x* axis and thus we need to check for negative values of **fSpeed**!

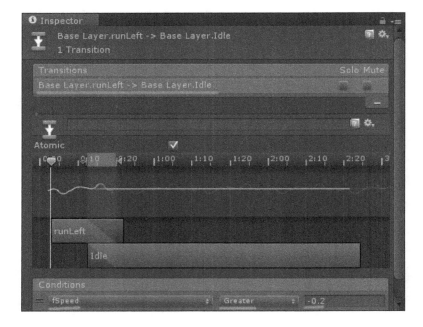

8. For the Jump animation, we use the **bJump** parameter. Create a transition from **Idle** to **Jump** and set **bJump** to **true** as its entering condition, as shown in the following screenshot:

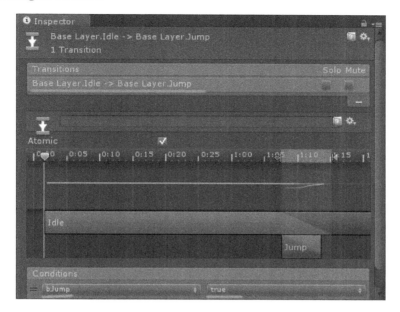

9. As for the exit transition, create a new one back from **Jump** to **Idle** and set **bJump** to **false** as its condition. You can refer to the following screenshot:

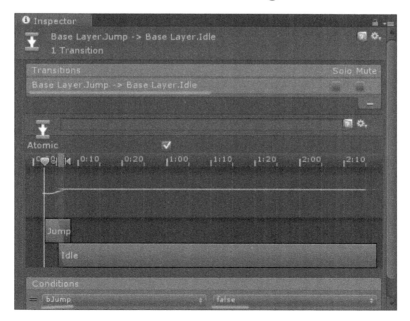

10. Repeat the same operations connecting **runRight** and **runLeft** to **Jump** to complete the task.

How it works...

With the Animator updated, the character now triggers the right running animations depending on its direction and a jump pose upon jumping. For the prototype, we don't need anything more than this.

Adding collectibles to the game level

Running on platforms is not enough for the prototype; we need to provide a player with a goal. Let's say that our prototype level is complete once the player has gathered a number of collectibles that we randomly scatter in the level.

To achieve that, we add a few lines to the PlatManager script and create a new prefab to be instantiated as our collectible game object.

Getting ready

Open the PlatManager script in **Monodevelop** and be ready to add the lines described here.

How to do it...

1. We need two extra variables to make the collectibles: a public Transform to store the reference to the collectible prefab and a private one to instantiate it. Do this by adding the following lines to the script:

```
public Transform collectPref;
private Transform collectible;
```

2. Next we create a new function called TossCollectible() that casts a random result to decide whether to instantiate a collectible on the next platform to be created in the level. Add the following lines to the script:

```
void TossCollectible(){
  float f = Random.Range(0f,1f);
  Debug.Log(f);
  if (f > 0.5){
    Vector3 v = new Vector3 (nextPos.x, nextPos.y + delta,
       0);
    collectible = (Transform)Instantiate(collectPref, v,
      Quaternion.identity);
  }
}
```

3. Now we can add a call to `TossCollectible()` when we instantiate a new platform in the level. What follows is the complete updated `FixedUpdate()` function, with the new lines highlighted:

```
void FixedUpdate(){
  UpdatePos();
  if(actualPlat != null && charX >
                  actualPlat.transform.position.x + delta){
      float strict = actualPlat.transform.position.x;
    prevPlat = actualPlat;
    actualPlat = null;
    SetScalesAndGaps();
    nextPos = new Vector3(strict + platScale.x + gap, yGap,
      charZ);
    nextPlat = (Transform)Instantiate(platBrick, nextPos,
        Quaternion.identity );
    nextPlat.localScale = platScale;
    TossCollectible();
  }
  if(actualPlat != null && charX <
                  actualPlat.transform.position.x - delta){
    float strict = actualPlat.transform.position.x;
    prevPlat = actualPlat;
    actualPlat = null;
    SetScalesAndGaps();
    nextPos = new Vector3(strict - platScale.x - gap, yGap,
      charZ);
    nextPlat = (Transform)Instantiate(platBrick, nextPos,
        Quaternion.identity );
    nextPlat.localScale = platScale;
    TossCollectible();
  }
  if(prevPlat != null){
    float strict = prevPlat.transform.position.x;
    if(charX > strict - delta && charX < strict + delta){
      Destroy(nextPlat.gameObject);
      nextPlat = null;
      actualPlat = prevPlat;
      prevPlat = null;
    }
  }
  if(nextPlat != null){
    float strict = nextPlat.transform.position.x;
    if(charX > strict - delta && charX < strict + delta){
      actualPlat = nextPlat;
```

```
            nextPlat = null;
            Destroy(prevPlat.gameObject);
          }
        }
    }
```

4. Next we need to edit the `Runner` script to manage the collisions between the character and the collectibles. Open the script in **Monodevelop**. We begin with declaring a new public `int` variable to store the number of items collected so far. We will display this data in the GUI, later. Add the following declaration at the top of the script:

```
public int collected;
```

5. In the `Start()` function, we initialize `collected` to 0, with one simple instruction. To make things more clear, we add the full `Start()` function as follows:

```
void Start () {
  charAnimator =
                  GameObject.Find("runner").
GetComponent<Animator>();
  horAcceleration = 4f;
  bIsTouch = false;
  jumpVel = new Vector3 (0,10,0);
  collected = 0;
}
```

6. Finally, we modify the `OnCollisionEnter()` function by adding a check for a second tag, named collectible, that we will create pretty soon. If we get a positive check with the tag, we can destroy the collectible instance and add 1 to the number of collected items. What follows is the updated `OnCollisionEnter()` function:

```
void OnCollisionEnter(Collision c){
  if(c.gameObject.tag == "platform"){
    bIsTouch = true;
    charAnimator.SetBool("bJump",false);
  }
  if(c.gameObject.tag == "collectible"){
    Destroy(c.gameObject);
    collected += 1;
  }
}
```

7. Now back to Unity, we need to create the prefab to be instantiated as the collectible. Let's start by adding **Sphere GameObject** to the scene. Scale it down to .35 on all axes and be sure that its position is reset to 0 on all axes.

8. Add any material you like to the sphere. We picked a red material, but anything you like will do the task.

9. Next, create a new prefab in the Prefabs folder of your project and name it **coll_prefab**. Then drag the sphere onto the prefab, as shown in the following screenshot:

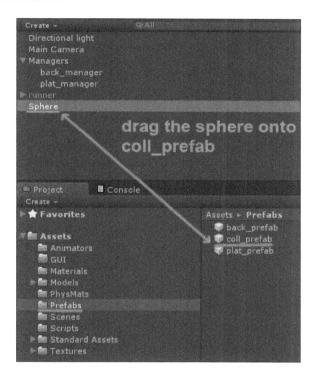

10. You can now delete **Sphere** from the scene. Select **coll_prefab** in the **Project** panel, then move to **Inspector**. In the Tag field, open the scrolling menu and add a new tag called **collectible**, as we did before, and set that tag for **coll_prefab**. You can refer to the following screenshot:

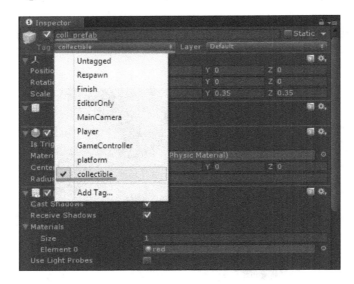

11. Last step: select **plat_manager** in **Scene**, then drag **coll_prefab** to the empty **Collect Pref** field, which represents the public variable we added to the **PlatManager** script. The following screenshot shows the operation:

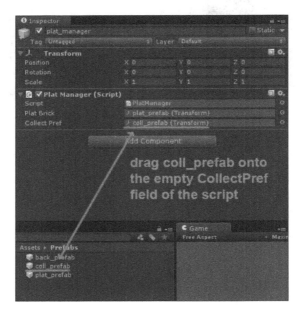

drag coll_prefab onto the empty CollectPref field of the script

12. You can now run the prototype and run around to collect items that appear above the platforms.

How it works...

The collectible objects are spawned with a random chance on platforms that get instantiated at runtime. Upon collision with the game character, they get destroyed and their count is increased by one.

There's more...

In the previous script, we used the `OnCollisionEnter()` function to detect when the character hits a collectible. Unity offers another method called `OnTriggerEnter()` that detects when two objects collide without generating a collision. The `OnTriggerEnter()` function is useful when you don't want two colliding objects to physically react upon collision. You can check out this link for a description of the difference between `OnCollisionEnter()` and `OnTriggerEnter()`: `http://answers.unity3d.com/questions/790724/what-is-the-difference-between-oncollisionenter-an.html`.

To complete our working prototype we need to add a control for the game camera so it follows the character. There is already a camera in the scene called **Main Camera**, so we will take advantage of it.

Camera setup and controls

Select **Main Camera** in **Scene**. We need to set it up and add a script to have it follow the character.

How to do it...

1. With **MainCamera** selected in **Scene**, move to the **Inspector** panel and access the **Camera** settings. Be sure that the **Field Of Vision**, **Far**, and **Near** clipping planes are set as shown in the following screenshot:

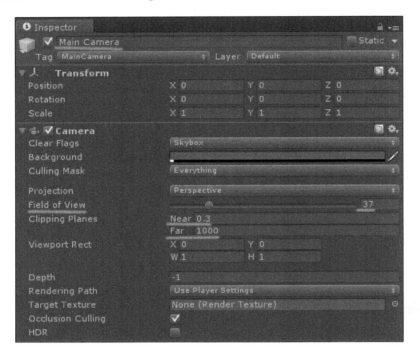

2. Now create a new C# script in the **Scripts** folder, name it **Camera Control** and open it in **Monodevelop**.

3. In the script, we set a reference to the character and in the Update() function we align the camera position with that of the character.

   What follows is the code for the script:

```csharp
using UnityEngine;
using System.Collections;

public class CameraControl : MonoBehaviour {

    public int distance;
    private Transform follow;
```

```
// Use this for initialization
void Start () {

    follow = GameObject.Find("runner").GetComponent<Transform>();
}

// Update is called once per frame
void Update () {

    Vector3 v = new Vector3 (follow.position.x, follow.position.y,
distance);
    transform.position = v;
    }
}
```

4. Next, we save the script and move back to Unity. Drag the script from the **Project** panel onto the **Main Camera** in the scene.

5. Set the **Distance** public variable in **Inspector** to a value you like. We picked a value of -15 to begin with. Check out the following screenshot that illustrates this:

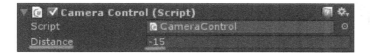

How it works...

This camera simply keeps the same character *x* and *y*, so the character itself is always at the center of the camera focus.

Please take into consideration that this script could be improved, for example, by allowing the player to look a bit ahead of the character before taking a leap. To delve more into the properties of Cameras in Unity, you can refer to the manual at `http://docs.unity3d.com/Manual/class-Camera.html`.

There's more...

In case you didn't do it yet, we recommend you add a **Directional light** to your scene so materials will look better on screen. You should know how to do that: from the top menu, navigate to **GameObject** | **Create Other** | **Directional Light**, as shown in the following screenshot:

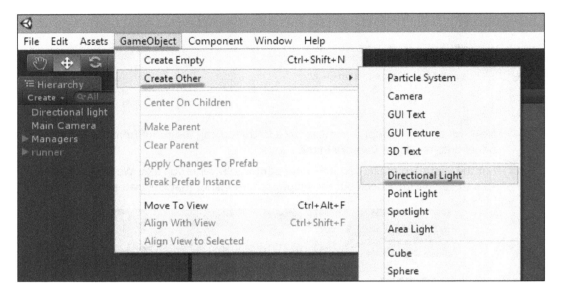

Now you can rotate the directional light using the gizmo as you see fit for your taste. Being a **Directional Light**, it will cast its rays independently from its actual position and distance from the character.

6
Game Scenes and the Graphic Interface

In this chapter, we will cover the following recipes:

- ▶ The game manager
- ▶ Loading a new scene at runtime
- ▶ Setting game exit conditions – character death
- ▶ Setting game exit conditions – goals met
- ▶ Using OnGUI() to display game data
- ▶ Displaying the number of collected items
- ▶ Game Won and Game Over

Introduction

Projects in Unity can be structured as collections of scenes, and scenes can be thought of as the different screens that are displayed while the game runs.

Upon launching, a game generally starts with a so-called main screen or home screen. This screen displays the relevant options to interact with the game. There is usually a **Play** button to launch the game, a button to edit game options such as audio and graphics, another button to launch a multiplayer session, and so on.

In this example, the home screen will be a scene in the Unity project, and each stage of the actual game will be a scene of its own, such as the **Game Won** and **Game Lost** screens. The following diagram shows the screen flow of our prototype:

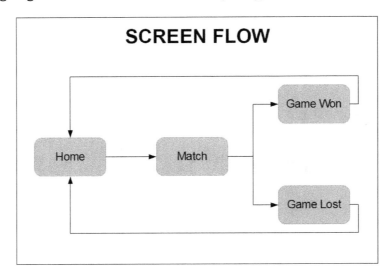

Scenes and their contents are loaded when required at runtime through scripting. When a scene is loaded, all the game objects and components that were saved in that scene when creating the game are loaded as well.

On the other hand, when the scene is unloaded, all game objects that were in that scene are destroyed, so a problem may arise. As a game runs, a collection of data about the player's actions and achievements is made, for example, the level they are playing, how they are performing, whether they edited any game option, and the like.

If game objects in the scenes are destroyed upon switching from one scene to another, how do we keep track of this data from the start to the end of the game?

Video games are usually designed as so-called **Finite state machines**. Finite state machines are a technique to restructure complex processes into a collection of states. Each state describes a specific condition that the process may enter, and it interacts with other states by getting and passing small pieces of information to them.

Each state is thus a sort of black box that autonomously gets data, processes it, and then sends it to another state, with no state knowing what the other states actually do.

The advantage of this approach when designing software, such as video games, is that if you need to make heavy modifications to an important game function, you just have to edit the state that takes care of that function, without affecting the rest of your project.

With regard to the prototype we are building up, we plan to organize it as a finite state machine made up of different scripts that take care of each specific game state. So, we can get back to the beginning of this introduction: a finite state machine requires one object to be the manager that controls the flow of information and gives control to the appropriate state as the game runs. But we stated earlier that when a scene is unloaded, all game objects in that scene are destroyed. So how do we save the game manager?

Unity features two important methods, called `Application.LoadLevel()` and `DontDestroyOnLoad()`, that allow us to load new game scenes at runtime and prevent game objects from being destroyed upon loading a new scene.

`Application.LoadLevel()` is called to load a new scene at runtime. It accepts either a `string` parameter with the scene name or an `int` parameter for the scene index.

You can read more about the `Application.LoadLevel()` method by referring to the link `http://docs.unity3d.com/ScriptReference/Application.LoadLevel.html`.

`DontDestroyOnLoad()` takes a game object as a parameter and prevents that game object from being destroyed. More details about this method can be found at `http://docs.unity3d.com/ScriptReference/Object.DontDestroyOnLoad.html`.

In the following recipe, we create the game manager for the prototype and use it to switch between the main and the game scenes.

The game manager

To create the game manager functionality, we need a script to initialize a new scene and the state manager. We also need a second scene to be added to our project, to switch between scenes (named **Home** and **Game**). Another script is required to create a button that sends the application from the home scene to the game scene. Finally, we need a game object to attach the scripts to, which we are preserving as we switch between scenes. Let's get to work!

Getting ready

Open your project in Unity. We begin by adding a new script to the `Scripts` folder.

How to do it...

1. Access the `Scripts` folder in the **Project** panel and create a new C# script. Name the script `StateManager`.
2. Double-click on the file to open it in **Monodevelop**.

3. Add the following lines to the script:

```
using UnityEngine;
using System.Collections;
public class StateManager : MonoBehaviour {
   private static StateManager instance
   public static StateManager Instance
   {
     get
     {
       if(instance == null)
       {
         instance = new
   GameObject("StateManager").AddComponent<StateManager>
         ();
       }
       return instance;
     }
   }
   public void OnApplicationQuit()
   {
     instance = null;
   }
   public void StartState()
   {
     Debug.Log ("New scene is being created...");
   }
}
```

4. Save the script.

5. Save the scene we built so far and name it `level_01`. As we haven't mentioned this before, we advise you to create a new folder in the **Project** panel before saving, and name it `Scenes`. Use this folder to save the `level_01` game scene and any other game scene you may create.

6. From the top menu, navigate to **File** | **NewScene** to create a new empty game scene.

7. Save this game scene too with the name `home`.

8. From the top menu, navigate to **GameObject** | **Create Empty**. We've added a screenshot showing this in case you don't remember how to do it:

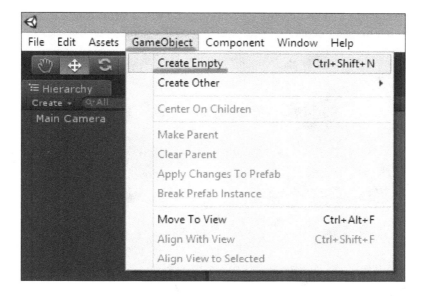

9. Name this object `game_starter` from the **Hierarchy** panel.

10. Now create a new C# script and name it the same as the object we will attach it to—`GameStarter`.

11. Open the script in **Monodevelop**. First, we need a function to create a button with a label on the screen so that we can launch the `lev_01` game scene at runtime. Add the following lines to the script:

```
void OnGUI(){
  if(GUI.Button(new Rect (120, 120, 150, 30), "Start Game"))
  {
    StartGame();
  }
}
```

In the previous piece of code, we call a `StartGame()` function on pressing the button. We need to add this function to the script with the following lines:

```
void StartGame(){
  print("starting game...");
  DontDestroyOnLoad(StateManager.Instance);
  StateManager.Instance.StartState();
}
```

Now drag the **GameStart** script onto the GameStarter game object, inside the home scene of your project.

12. Run the game. You should see an empty scene with a **Start Game** button, as shown in the following screenshot. Press it to launch the game scene we have built so far.

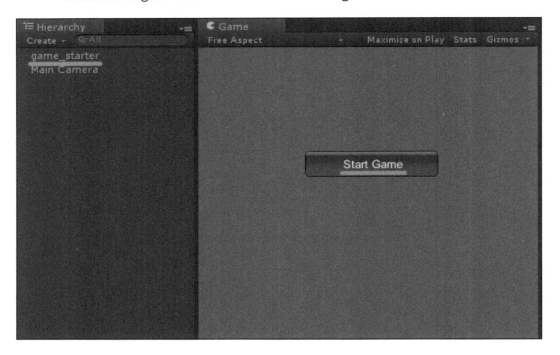

How it works...

The home scene is the launching game screen of our prototype. The script attached to the GameStarter game object in the scene creates a button. Upon pressing this button, an instance of a game object with the `StateManager` script is added to the scene. The `DontDestroyOnLoad()` method takes care of preventing this script from being destroyed whenever we switch between game scenes.

There's more...

State machines is a fascinating topic for anyone interested in science in general. For game developers, even more for AI developers, it is a must! We recommend digging into this matter, starting with `http://en.wikipedia.org/wiki/Finite-state_machine`.

Loading a new scene at runtime

With a state manager that handles multiple games scenes, we can now move on to loading those scenes in the game. In the next recipe, we add the `level_1` scene to our project and modify the code so that `level_01` is loaded upon pressing the interface button displayed in the **game_starter** scene.

Getting ready

We keep up from where we left at the end of previous recipe. Just be sure that you have the **game_starter** scene loaded in your project and that an empty game object called **game_starter** is present in the scene, with the **GameStart** script attached to it.
You can refer to the following screenshot:

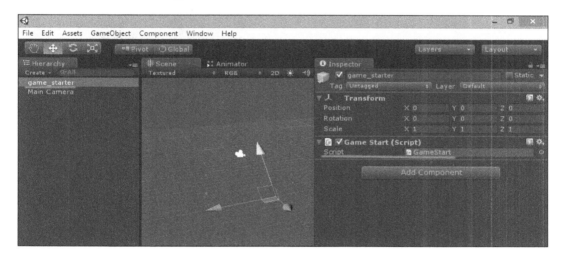

How to do it...

1. With **Game Start** scene loaded in Unity, navigate to **File | Build Settings** to open the **Build Settings** panel.

2. Click on **AddCurrent** to add the loaded scene to the game build, as shown in this screenshot:

3. Now load the scene called `level_01`. Refer to the following screenshot to check out the scene that contains the right game object:

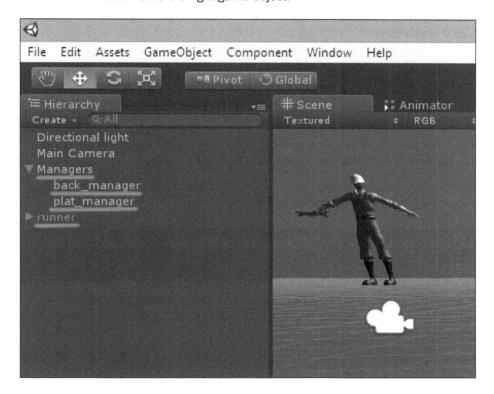

4. Add this scene too to the **Build Settings** panel, just as we did before.

5. With a second scene added to the prototype, we need to enter the instructions to actually load `level_01` when the button in the **Game Start** scene is pressed. Open the **GameStart** script in **Monodevelop** and modify the `GameStart()` function as follows:

```
void GameStart(){
  print("starting game...");

  DontDestroyOnLoad(StateManager.Instance);
  Application.LoadLevel("level_1");");
  StateManager.Instance.StartState();
}
```

6. Save the script and go back to Unity.

7. Load **Game Start** scene into the Editor.

How it works...

If you run the game now, it should begin with Game Start scene, which only consists of an empty scene and a button.

When you press the button, `level_01` is loaded and the game begins.

When working with Unity, you generally build up a project of several scenes. Each scene should be designed to host a relevant game phase such as the launching screen, the actual game levels, a "game over" scene, or anything you may need for your game.

It is important to learn how to switch between these scenes efficiently and how to create them in such a way that they remain manageable as the project grows.

`DontDestroyOnLoad()` and `Application.LoadLevel()` are the most important functions used to actually build up such a system.

Setting game exit conditions – character death

The prototype still lacks a **Heads-Up Display** (**HUD**) completely. Heads-up display is a term used to refer to the collection of game information that is available for the player on the screen.

Health bars, lives indicators, speed references, and position references are all examples of common game HUD elements.

For this prototype, we plan to display two types of information on the screen: the number of collectibles gathered from the beginning of the match, and the number of available lives before the game ends. It's not by chance that we chose these two elements, as they are linked to the relevant variables to decide whether the player is winning or losing the game.

Before we can work on a game interface, however, we need to define the two exit conditions for our game: the "game over" and the "game won" conditions.

The plan is to have the game sending a **Game Over** message if the player loses three lives, and a **Game Won** message if they gather five collectibles. Let's begin with setting the condition for losing the game.

Getting ready

Let's say we want the player to lose a life whenever the character falls from a platform. This can be set up by adding a few lines to our **PlatManager** script.

How to do it...

1. Open **PlatManager** in **Monodevelop**.

2. In the `Start()` function, we already have a reference to the game character thanks to this line:

```
thisChar =
    GameObject.Find("runner").GetComponent<Transform>();
```

With this reference already set, we add a public variable to count the lives available to the player:

```
public int lives;
```

3. We also need a public `float` variable to store a reference value for our character's position. We will use it to check whether the character is falling:

```
harpublic float yOffsetC
```

4. We now can set the value of lives and `yOffset` to their default values. Add these lines to the `Start()` function of the script:

```
lives = 3;
yOffset = -37;
```

5. Now scroll down to the `FixedUpdate()` function and add the following `if()` statement at the end of it. The `if()` statement check whether the character is falling down and, in case it does, it moves it back above the platform closest to it.

```
if(thisChar.position.y < -yOffset){

    lives -= 1;

    Vector3 v = new Vector3 (0,0,0);
    if(nextPlat){
      v = nextPlat.position;
    }
    else{
      v = actualPlat.position;
    }

    v.y += 40;
    thisChar.position = v;
}
```

How it works...

The `if()` statement in `FixedUpdate()` checks at every frame the character's *y* position. If this value goes beyond the threshold provided with `yOffset` (`-37` in our case), it means that the character is falling, so the script takes `1` away from the number of available lives and moves the character back to a safe position.

Setting game exit conditions – goals met

To set the winning conditions for the level, we need to count the items collected and check that value against a default number of items we want the level to end with. Once the number of items collected equals the goal, the player receives a message.

This is the topic of our next recipe.

Getting ready

We have already counted the number of items collected in the `runner` script, through the `collected int` variable. Thus we can take advantage of the code we already implemented and improve it to manage the additional functionality.

How to do it...

1. Open the `runner` script in Monodevelop. In the upper section with the variable declaration, modify the declaration for `collected`, as shown here:

   ```
   public int collected, levelGoal;
   ```

2. In the `Start()` function, add the initialization for `levelGoal` with the value of 5:

   ```
   collected = 0;
   levelGoal= 5;
   ```

3. In the `Update()` function, add the following lines to check whether the winning conditions are met, and send a message to the player if they are met:

   ```
   if(collected == levelGoal){
     Time.timeScale = 0;
     Debug.Log("level complete!");
   }
   ```

4. If you try the game now, you should see that upon collecting five items, the game stops and the **Level complete!** message is displayed in the **Console**.

How it works...

The logic is pretty easy here; whenever the player collects an item, the number of total items collected is increased by one. When this number equals the goal value we set for the level, the game ends.

In this book, we will gradually work to improve the feedback provided for the player and the game flow.

Using OnGUI() to display game data

As we are gathering game data about the player's performance, we can display that information on screen to the player's advantage.

Unity offers a collection of functions and constructs to display game data on the screen and create the **Graphic User Interface** (**GUI**) of your game. `OnGUI()` is an important method available in Unity and used to create and control GUI elements to be displayed on the screen. Inside the function, it is possible to put lines of code that create interface controls such as text fields, buttons, and sliders at runtime. We advise you to check out the following link:

`http://docs.unity3d.com/Manual/gui-Basics.html`

In this recipe, we will use the `OnGUI()` function to display game data. We will create a script to access the number of lives and the items collected, and display them on the screen.

We need a couple of screenshots to be used as icons too, so get ready to follow our instructions.

Getting ready

The first step is to import the images to be used to display the information on the screen. The plan is to have a small character icon in the bottom-left corner for every available life, and an icon and a number in the top-right corner to display the number of collected items.

To display both of these pieces of information on screen we make use of a method called `Graphics.DrawTexture()`. It creates a rectangular area on the screen and draws a texture inside it. The texture to be displayed can be passed as a global **Texture** type variable. Several extra parameters can be set for the rectangle area, and their details have been explained in the manual available at `http://docs.unity3d.com/ScriptReference/Graphics.DrawTexture.html`.

Let's do it!

How to do it...

1. Access the `Texture` folder in your project and right-click anywhere inside the window to open the menu. Select **Import New Asset**, as shown in this screenshot:

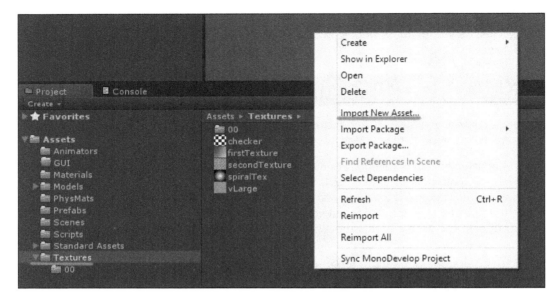

2. Select the images named **lifeIcon** and **collIcon** from the package provided with this book. Alternatively, you can create your own images to use. In that case, remember to save them in PNG format.

3. Select **lifeIcon** from the folder and check its **Alpha is Transparency** property, as shown in the following screenshot:

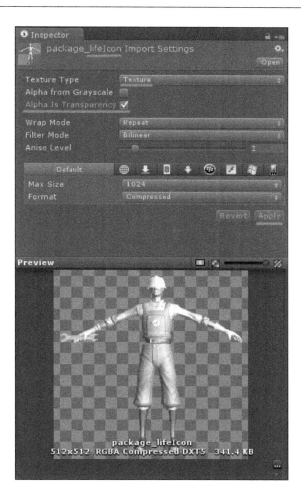

4. Repeat the operation to import and set up the **collIcon** PNG image.

5. Next, we create a new script in the `Scripts` folder and name it **GUI** as well. Then we open it in **Monodevelop**.

6. We begin by declaring two public variables of the **Texture** type to store the references to these pics, and two private variables to store the references to the scripts where we take the data to be displayed on screen. Add the following lines to the script:

    ```
    public Texture lifeIcon;
    public Texture collIcon;
    private PlatManager platScript;
    private Runner runScript;
    ```

In the `Start()` function, as usual, we initialize the variables by getting the `plat_manager` and `runner` references. The following instructions must be added to the script:

```
// Use this for initialization
void Start () {
platScript =
  GameObject.Find("plat_manager").GetComponent<PlatManager>();
  runScript = GameObject.Find ("runner").GetComponent<Runner>();
}
```

7. The next step is to use the `OnGUI()` function to draw the icons on the screen. We use a `for` loop to draw a life icon for each available life. Add the following lines to the script:

```
void OnGUI(){
  for(int i=0; i<platScript.lives; i++){
    Graphics.DrawTexture(new Rect(10 + (60*i), 600, 50,
      50), lifeIcon);
  }
}
```

How it works...

The logic to display a number of icons based on a numeric parameter is pretty straightforward; we loop between the number of lives in the `OnGUI()` function itself. As `OnGUI()` is called at least once per frame (actually, it can be called more than once per cycle), the number of icons displayed on screen is always updated with the actual number of lives.

There's more...

The `OnGUI()` function is called before the GUI elements on the screen are rendered, and after events such as an input from the player (mouse, buttons, and so on). As a consequence, `OnGUI()` may be called several times during an update cycle. For that reason, it is not advisable to put game controls in the `OnGUI()` function. There is an interesting article about this available at `http://answers.unity3d.com/questions/197798/clarification-on-updates-physics-events-order-and.html`.

Display the number of collected items

We need to draw an icon for the collected items and text to show the player the updated number of items collected. We put this information in the top-right corner, close to the spherical icon.

Getting ready

Open the `GUI` script in **Monodevelop** and be ready to follow our instructions.

How to do it...

1. Add these lines to the `OnGUI()` function:

    ```
    void OnGUI(){
      for(int i=0; i<platScript.lives; i++){
        Graphics.DrawTexture(new Rect(30 + (60*i), 700, 50,
          50), lifeIcon);
    }

        Graphics.DrawTexture(new Rect(880, 28, 30, 30),
          collIcon);
    }
    ```

2. To display the text telling the player how many items they have collected, we need to do some extra work. First of all, create a new `TextMesh` in the game scene by navigating to **GameObject | Create Other | 3D Text**, as shown in this screenshot:

3. Name this text **collText** and drag it onto **MainCamera** in the scene so it becomes a child of **MainCamera**. We do this so that once we have set the desired position of the text with regard to the camera, the text moves along with it, keeping its relative position.

4. Set the position of the text in the World Space. In the following screenshot, we provide the values we set for our prototype, considering the fact that we are displaying it with our viewport set as **1024 x 768** and **Standalone**:

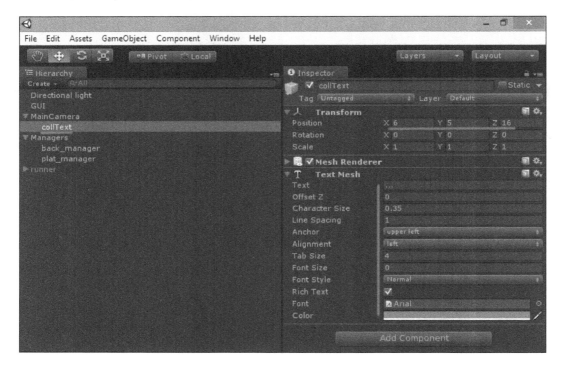

5. Go back to the **GUI** script in **Monodevelop**. We need a few additions to it. There are actually two ways to display that text on the screen. One way is to add a public variable to the script to store a reference to the text in the scene and drag the **3D Text** game object into the variable.

   The other way is to create two private variables: one to store a reference to the camera, and another to store the reference to the 3D Text attached to that camera. Then, in the `Start()` function, we instantiate the two variables to access the content we are searching for.

   The first approach is easier and more straightforward, so we pick that. Add the following variable declaration at the beginning of the **GUI** script:

   ```
   public TextMesh tm;
   ```

6. Now go to the `Update()` function and add the following line to it:

```
void Update () {
  tm.text = runScript.collected + " / 5";
}
```

7. The last step consists of dragging the **3D Text** game object into the `tm` slot in the script attached to **GUI** from the **Inspector** panel, as shown in this screenshot:

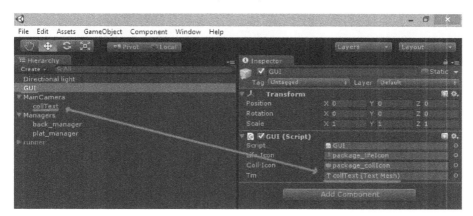

8. If you play the game now, the icons representing the available lives are displayed in the bottom-left corner of the screen, while the icon and the number of items collected are displayed on the top-right corner. You may need to resize the game scene or the numeric parameters to display them correctly. The following screenshot shows the output we get on the screen:

How it works...

Our approach to display the text on screen is pretty efficient; we use a single public variable to store the reference to **3D Text**, and set the text we want to be displayed in the Update() function using the tm.text = runScript.collected + " / 5" line. We made the 3D text a child of **MainCamera** so it moves along the screen, keeping its relative position to the camera.

Game Won and Game Over

Before we end this chapter, we need to do a last thing: add the **Game Won** and **Game Over** screens to the prototype. At this point, our project consists of two screens: the home screen, where the game starts, and level_01, our actual game stage. Now we are going to add two more scenes: a **Game Over** screen to send the application to if the player loses, and a **Game Won** scene to be displayed if the player completes the game goals. For each new screen, we need a new scene and a script. In each screen we add, we plan to display a message and a button to send the application back to the **Home** screen.

Let's get to work!

Getting ready

Save your project and the scenes you built so far, which should be two: the **Home** screen and level_01.

How to do it...

1. From the top menu, create a new scene by navigating to **File** | **New Scene** (or press *Ctrl + N*).

2. Name this scene game_won.

3. Add **3D Text** to the scene as we did before, by going to **GameObject** | **Create Other** | **3D Text**.

4. Select the text in the scene and name it **message_won**.

5. With the text selected in the scene, move to the **Inspector** to access its properties. Set the values as what you consider fit for your camera and scene settings. The following screenshot shows the settings I used with my game camera:

6. If you want more than one text line in the message, you can do so in two ways.

   You can duplicate the **3D Text** in the scene, change its text (and its font size and style too), set the position for the second line, and then make it a child of the first line, or add a script to the **3D Text** game object with a line like this:

   ```
   public class Texter : MonoBehaviour {
     private string wonText;
     void Start () {
       wonText = "Congratulations \n Level Complete";
       GetComponent<TextMesh>().text = wonText;
     }
   }
   ```

   The \n operator is used to tell the parser that it must go to a new line.

7. Let's also add to this script the code used to display a button to send the application back to the **Home** screen.

8. Please add the following lines to the `OnGUI()` section of the script:

```
void OnGUI() {
  if(GUI.Button(new Rect (120, 120, 150, 30), "Home")){
    Application.loadedLevel("home");
  }
}
```

9. The operations to make the **Game Over** screen are exactly the same as those required to make the **Game Won** screen. Create the scene, name it `game_lost`, add the **3D Text** to it, and drag a script onto the text. The code to be added is as follows:

```
public class Texter : MonoBehaviour {

  private string lostText;
  void Start () {
    lostText = "Too bad, you run out of lives! \n Play
      again";
    GetComponent<TextMesh>().text = lostText;
  }
  void OnGUI() {
    if(GUI.Button(new Rect (120, 120, 150, 30), "Home")){
      Application.loadedLevel("home");
    }
  }
}
```

How it works...

We keep up with the logic we implemented so far. Each game state sends the application to a different scene. Each scene handles itself autonomously and provides options to send the application to the next state depending on the player's input. Should we need to change anything from any state, our changes won't affect the other states.

There's more...

The 3D Text game object is a newcomer with the latest Unity version, and it is a welcome addition for many HUD- and interface-related needs. Refer to `http://docs.unity3d.com/Manual/class-TextMesh.html` for a detailed description of the control parameters of `TextMesh`.

7
Improving Your Gaming Experience

In this chapter, we will cover the following recipes:

- ▶ Importing audio clips
- ▶ The Audio Source component
- ▶ Coding audio
- ▶ Instantiating Particle Systems at runtime
- ▶ Game options—audio volume
- ▶ Game options—toggling audio
- ▶ Playing video clips in the scene

It seems we have enough dough to work with! Let's start by adding sounds to the prototype.

Introduction

In this chapter, we add details and extra functionality to our prototype, starting with audio. Audio in video games is, in our opinion, a sort of ambiguous matter. On one side, audio is an important part of any video game, as it is complements its graphics to immerse the player into the actual game world and game action. There are so many games that are mostly popular because of their soundtrack, and there is good literature on this subject too. If you'd like to delve into the theory of audio in games, you can check out an interesting read about the diegesis theory, available at `http://devmag.org.za/2012/04/19/video-game-audio-diegesis-theory-2/`.

On the other side, audio in video games is generally taken care of by an audio designer— a contractor who is rarely a permanent member of the development team. Most of the time, the audio designer starts working on a project towards its end. The main negative consequence of this industry habit is that audio rarely gets the attention it would require during the preproduction phase of a project.

The rise of mobile gaming didn't help the cause of audio designers, as the casual style of mobile gaming, which encourages playing everywhere while doing anything, tends to make players prefer disabling the game audio entirely.

That said, we begin this chapter with two recipes about managing audio files in Unity.

The other main topic we will discuss in this chapter is particle effects. Particle effects are bits of graphics that are displayed on screen to improve the visual appeal of a video game. Explosions, smoke puffs, glitters, and rainfall are all examples of particle effects applied to video games.

Besides the visual impact, particles may also be very important from a design perspective, as they provide a tool to improve the player's feedback on the consequences of their own game actions. Well-designed particle effects can definitely help a player understand whether they are performing well or badly, while playing.

In the second part of this chapter, we will show you how to create particle effects in Unity and how to implement them in the prototype.

Importing audio clips

Audio in Unity is managed according to the same easy philosophy that is applied to importing and managing graphics. The most common audio formats such as MPEG, WAV, AIFF, and MP3 are supported, and once imported, audio clips can be easily configured in the **Inspector** panel.

With regard to the file format, the general rule is to use large WAV files for background music and small MP3 files for sound effects.

The compression setting is the other basic configuration of an audio clip in Unity, as Unity allows audio clips to be set as **Native** or **Compressed**. By setting a clip as **Native**, we ensure that the clip won't need to be decoded at runtime. The file will be larger, but it sounds nicer and won't slow down the application once it gets played. The native setting is recommended for short sound effects that are usually imported as MP3 files, and thus not recompressed once they get imported in Unity.

Setting a clip as **Compressed** results in a smaller project file, but that file must be decoded before playing the sound at runtime. Decompressing audio files many times per frame would impair the performance of an application. To prevent this, it is recommended to use compressed audio files for the game backgrounds and music carpets, which don't change so often while playing. Moreover, to prevent the compression from affecting the quality of audio, it is also recommended that you compress only native file formats such as wav and aiff. Refer to the following diagram to know more about the use of compressed and uncompressed audio files in Unity:

	COMPRESSED	UN-COMPRESSED
MUSIC	wav, aiff	mp3
SOUND FX	-	

For those of you specifically interested in digital audio, there is a detailed introduction to this subject available at `http://www.jiscdigitalmedia.ac.uk/guide/an-introduction-to-digital-audio`.

Importing audio works like all other imports we have done so far. We provided selection clips to be used for the recipes. If you like to use yours, just be sure to have a small MP3 file for the sound effect and a larger (possibly looped) WAV or MP3 file for the background music.

Getting ready

Open your project in Unity and load the actual game scene. Then create a new folder in the **Project** panel and name it `Audio`. We will use this folder to store the audio clips to be imported.

How to do it...

1. Access the **Project** panel in Unity and right-click on the **Audio** folder. Select **Import New Asset** from the menu.
2. Select the **MP3** file named `sfx_01` and click on **Import** in the **Import** window.
3. With the clip selected in the **Project** panel, move to the **Inspector** window and check the **Audio Format** parameter is set to **Native**. We do this because the audio clip is already a compressed MP3 file, so there's no need to compress it again!.

4. We also want to set the sound as a 2D sound. In our prototype, the character can't move on the z axis, and the camera follows the character as it runs left or right. As the distance between the character and the camera doesn't change while playing, there is no point in burdening the CPU with extra calculations to determine the distance between the camera and the game action at runtime.

5. We also select the **Load into memory** option to improve performance. This sound effect will be loaded in the memory when the application starts, and thus won't require any additional loading operation at runtime. Should a project get larger in size (from a memory management perspective), it could make sense saving that amount of memory and letting the file be loaded at runtime when required by setting it as **Stream from Disc**.

The following screenshot displays the audio clip settings we explained so far.

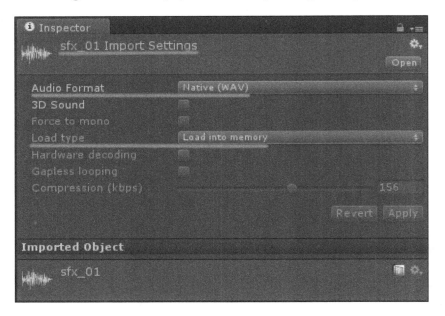

6. Now we import a larger file, and we will compress it in the **Inspector** window. Import a new asset; this time, pick the file named bkgd_01. We use a WAV file so that we have a better source to compress.

7. Set the clip properties in **Inspector**, as shown in the following screenshot. For better performance, we store the compressed file in the memory so that Unity doesn't need to decompress it at runtime.

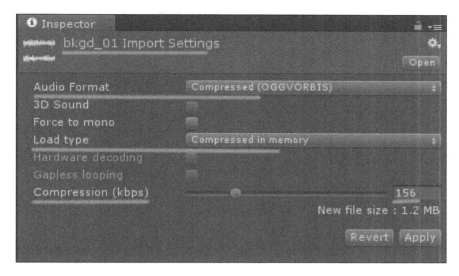

8. Don't forget to click on **Apply** in the **Inspector** panel to save the settings.

How it works...

These simple operations are all that's required to import and set up audio clips in Unity. Compressed files are smaller but require a decoding operation at runtime, which could, on the long run, slow down the application. Uncompressed files are larger but perform better at runtime. That said, we used a small, uncompressed MP3 file for the sound effects, and a large, compressed WAV file for the background music. Now that we have audio clips imported in the project, we can move on and add them to our game objects.

The Audio Source component

When a new scene is created in Unity, a **Main Camera** object is created as well, and included in the scene. This camera is responsible, by default, for displaying the actual game scene when we press the **Play** button in the Unity Editor. Among the components the camera comes attached with by default, there is a component named **Audio Listener** (you can check it out in the **Inspector** panel). This component allows sounds to be heard by the player through the built-in speakers of their device or through a headset.

The **Audio Listener** constitutes the receiving half of the audio system implemented in Unity, the other half (the source half) being another Unity component called **Audio Source**. While the **Audio Listener** is generally attached to the main camera in the scene, **Audio Source** is attached to game objects in the scene that emit sounds, be they short sound effects or long, looped background music. In other words, to hear game sounds in Unity, you need to have at least one **Audio Listener** in the scene and (likely) several Audio Sources with an audio clip linked to them. Let's now see how the **Audio Source** component is attached to a game object.

Getting ready

Open the game scene in Unity.

How to do it...

1. Move to the **Project** panel and access the **Prefabs** folder, then drag **coll_prefab** into the game scene.
2. With **coll_prefab** selected in **Scene**, navigate to **Component | Audio | Audio Source**, as shown in this screenshot:

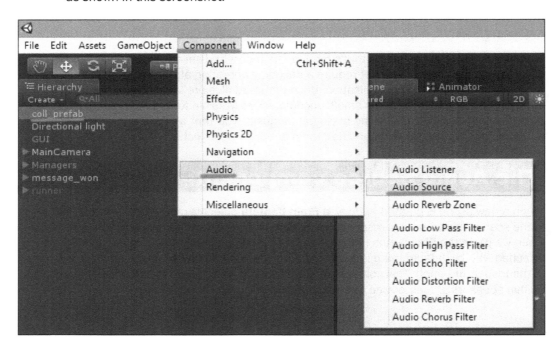

3. Ensure that **coll_prefab** is still selected in the scene. From the **Project** panel, access the **Audio** folder and drag **sfx_01** onto the **Audio Clip** slot of **Audio Source** in the **Inspector** window, as shown in the following screenshot:

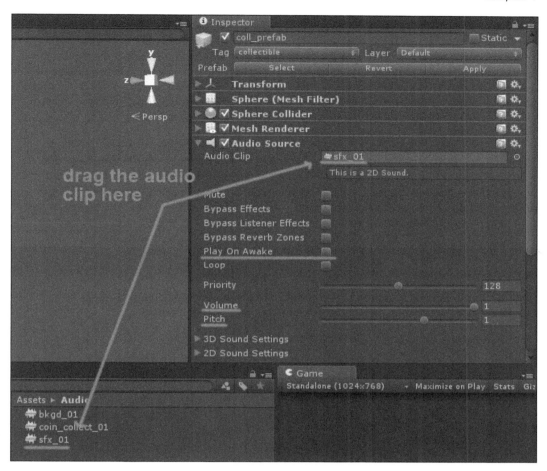

drag the audio
clip here

4. As for the parameters, we only take care of unflagging the **Play On Awake** option. With this option flagged, the clip would be played whenever a collectible is created in the game scene, which is not what we want for now. Instead, our plan is to play the sound effect when the character gets the collectible.

How it works...

The audio clip dragged into the **Audio Source** component is now ready to be played on our command. As previously stated, we plan to play this sound when the player collects an item. In the next recipe, we will show you how to code the audio clip to be played accordingly.

There's more...

There are two more components of the Audio System in Unity that are worth mentioning, for the sake of completeness. One of them is **Audio Filters**. This is a feature available only with Unity Pro, and it consists of additional audio components that can be attached to **Audio Source** or **Audio Listener** to apply special effects to sounds, such as reverberation, chorus, echo, and so on. More details about these effects are available at `http://docs.unity3d.com/Manual/class-AudioEffect.html`.

The other component is the reverb zone. This can be attached to an **Audio Source** to define a faraway area where that sound can't be heard, a closer area where the sound is heard according to a gradient based on distance, and a proximity area where the sound is fully audible. To know more about Reverb Zones, you can refer to `http://docs.unity3d.com/Manual/class-AudioReverbZone.html`.

Coding audio

With the **Audio Source** attached to the **collectible prefab**, the obvious idea would be to play the sound when a collision occurs between the character and the item.

This can be done by adding a few lines to the **Runner** script.

In the `OnCollisionEnter()` function of the script, we write this `if` statement to check whether the character hit a collectible:

```
if(c.gameObject.tag == "collectible"){
  Destroy(c.gameObject);
  collected += 1;
  Debug.Log(collected);
}
```

If we want the audio clip to be played when the character collides with a collectible, we can apparently put the following line inside the `if()` statement:

```
c.gameObject.audio.Play();
```

Unfortunately, we can't do that! If we did, the collectible game object would be destroyed the very moment it begins playing the sound, and the player would hear nothing.

This is a common problem, but there are many solutions to overcome it. The solution we provide is a creative way to achieve the result we want, and it involves using another important Unity asset we didn't mention yet.

Particle systems

To solve the problem of playing the audio and destroying the game object at the same time, we will use a particle system. A particle system is a complex game object that emits so-called particles in the game scene. Particle effects are largely used in video games for various graphic touches—game object trails, glitter, smoke, explosions, rain, snow, and so on.

Particles, by themselves, are multiple instances of (usually) tiny game objects with a mesh, transparent texture, and direction in the World Space. These particles sprout from a component of the particle system called Emitter.

The Emitter emits a large number of particles over time, and then these particles fly through the scene, according to several user-defined parameters. We can define the size and shape of the area where the particles tend to crowd as they emerge; the lifetime of individual particles before they get destroyed; the change in shape, color, or direction of the particles as they fly through the scene; and much more.

Using particle systems in Unity is not very hard, provided you have the right assets and a clear idea of the result you want to achieve. In the following recipe, we will show you how to add and set up a particle system to be used when the player collects an item.

The particle system we are going to create covers two purposes. The first purpose is to enrich the visuals and the feedback coming from the game. A nice puff that appears when the collectible is gathered by the character helps the player to understand what just happened, and will hopefully make them smile for what they've done!

The other purpose of the particle system is to play the sound we want to be heard by the player when a collectible is gathered, and then destroy itself. To do this, we first need to move **Audio Source** and its attached clip from the collectible prefab to the the new particle system we are about to create.

Getting ready

Let's begin by editing **coll_prefab** and removing **Audio Source** from it. Open the project scene and be ready to follow our instructions.

How to do it...

1. To remove a component from a prefab, we begin by dragging the prefab itself into the scene. Drag **coll_prefab** from the **Prefabs** folder in the **Project** panel into the scene.

2. Select **coll_prefab** in the scene and move to the **Inspector** window. Scroll down in the list of components until you find **Audio Source**. then click on the small wheel icon to open the component menu. Select **Remove Component**, as shown in this screenshot:

3. Click on the **Apply** button to save the edits as shown in the following screenshot:

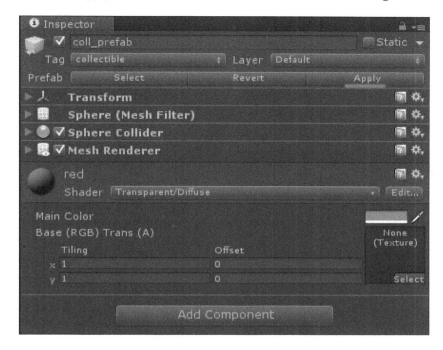

4. You can now remove **coll_prefab** from the scene.

5. Add a new game object from the scene. From the menu, navigate to **GameObject** | **Create Other** | **Particle System**, as shown in the following screenshot:

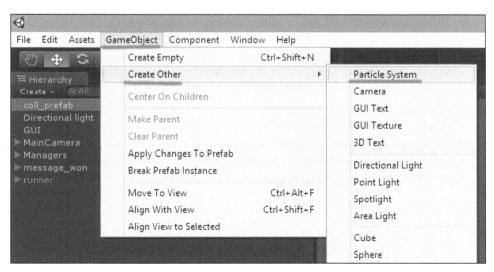

6. Name the particle system **sparkles**.

7. The particle system in the scene should be already emitting particles. If you now move to the **Inspector** window, you will see the many submenus that are available to fine-tune the particle system in the scene. Let's just take care of the most relevant submenus here.

   The **Particle System** menu contains general settings for the particle system and several parameters related to shape, lifetime, color, and speed of the particles when they are first created. You can set this group of parameters as shown in this screenshot:

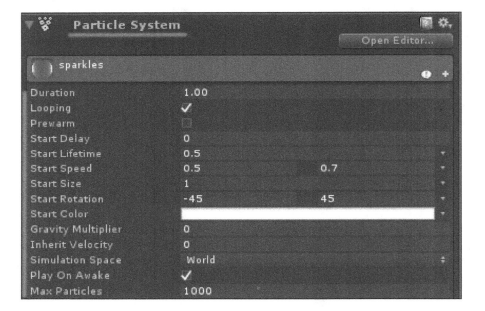

8. The **Emission** submenu is meant to control the number of particles we want to be emitted per second or the number of particles that must be emitted with each burst. Let's use a value of 1 in the **Rate** settings, for this.

9. Now click on the small **+** icon on the right side to add a burst of 15 particles, as shown in the next screenshot.

10. The **Shape** menu is used to set the shape of the emission in the 3D world. There are a number of predefined shapes, and there is also the ability to define a custom mesh to be used as the shape. In our case, we pick a **Sphere** shape of **Radius** 0.01.

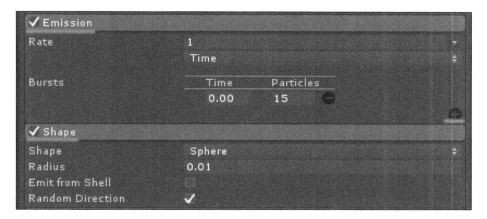

11. The **Color** menu allows us to control the change of the particles' color over time. It also allows us to set color opacity over time. This feature, in particular, is useful for us to create that puff effect we mentioned, because we actually want the puffs to progressively disappear by getting more and more transparent as time passes by.

12. Check the **Color over Lifetime** box. Then click on the white bar to open **Gradient Editor**, and apply the settings displayed in this screenshot:

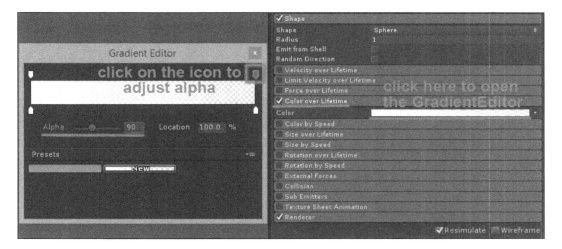

13. The **Renderer** menu allows to customize the shape and material of individual particles and set whether particles should have and receive shadows, among the others. Before we set it up, let's import a texture to make a material for the particle system we are creating.

14. In the **Project** panel, access the **Textures** folder and import **Texture** named `tex_ps` to the project.

15. Set **Texture** in the **Inspector** window, as shown in the following screenshot:

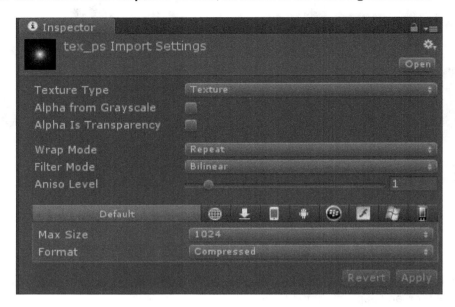

16. Now create a new material in the **Materials** folder and name it **mat_ps**. Drag **tex_ps** into the the texture slot of the material and set **Shader** for this material as **Particles\ Additive**, as shown in this screenshot:

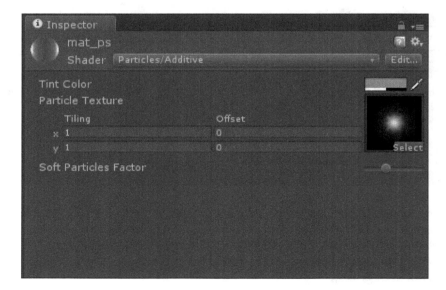

17. Finally, we can finish editing **Renderer** of our Particle System by dragging **mat_smoke** into the material slot in the **Renderer** menu of the Particle System, as shown in the following screenshot:

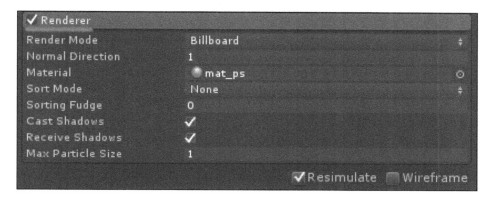

18. There are a couple of more steps before we end this recipe. The first is to add an **Audio Source** to the particle system to play the **sfx_01** clip. We did this operation in the previous recipe, so we have to repeat those same steps. Add the **Audio Source** to the particle systems and drag the **sfx_01** audio clip into it.

19. What we didn't do earlier but need to do now is to select the **Play On Awake** option in the **Audio Source** component. This way, the audio will be played the very moment the PS is created in the scene, which is what we want.

How it works...

A particle system is collection of components that are used to create graphic effects for your game scenes. It consists of a part called Emitter. This part emits tiny, flat meshes with a transparent texture, called particles. Particles fly through the game scene and behave according to a large number of parameters that set their movement, direction, duration, color, opacity, and so on.

There's more...

Particle systems are an important component of almost any video game, and once you get used to the settings the several submenus, they are very funny to experiment with! A thorough explanation of their many properties and uses goes beyond the scope of this manual, so you can to refer to the guide at `http://docs.unity3d.com/Manual/class-ParticleSystem.html` and to experiment a lot.

Instantiating a particle system at runtime

In this recipe, we take care of instantiating a particle system prefab in the place of a collected item that disappears, and also use the particle system to play the sound effect we set for this specific game event.

To achieve this, we need a new script and need to make some modifications to the **Runner** script, so let's begin.

Getting ready

Keep your project ready to add the new assets we need.

How to do it

1. Create a new C# script in the **Scripts** folder of your project and name it **PS_Manager**.

2. Edit the `Update()` function so that it contains the following lines. They tell the PS to destroy itself once the audio attached to it has finished playing:

    ```
    void Update () {
      if (!audio.isPlaying) {
        Destroy(this.gameObject);
      }
    }
    ```

3. Now open the **Runner** script in **Monodevelop**, if you did not open before.

4. To begin with, we need a public **GameObject** variable to store the reference to the particle system prefab we are going to create in the scene. Add the following line to the script:

    ```
    public GameObject ps;
    ```

5. Add this line to the collectible's `if()` statement inside the `OnCollisionEnter()` function. It takes care of creating the PS in the place of the collectible, which can then be destroyed:

    ```
    Instantiate(ps, c.transform.position, Quaternion.identity);
    ```

6. For extra clarity, we are displaying the complete, updated `OnCollisionEnter()` function of the **Runner** script:

    ```
    void OnCollisionEnter(Collision c){

      if(c.gameObject.tag == "platform"){
        bIsTouch = true;
        charAnimator.SetBool("bJump",false);
      }
    ```

```
if(c.gameObject.tag == "collectible"){
    Instantiate(ps, c.transform.position,
      Quaternion.identity);
    GameObject.Destroy(c.gameObject);
    collected += 1;
  }
}
```

7. Save both **Runner** and **PS_Manager** in **Monodevelop**.

8. Drag **PS_Manager** from the **Project** panel onto the PS on the scene.

9. Now create a new prefab in the **Prefabs** folder and name it **coll_ps_prefab**. Then drag the particle system from the scene onto **coll_ps_prefab** in the **Project** panel. With that done, the particle system in the scene can be removed.

10. The last step is to select the **runner** character in **Scene** to access its **Runner** script in the **Inspector** panel, and from there, drag **coll_ps_prefab** into the **Ps** slot we created, with the ps public variable.

    You can refer to the following screenshot that shows the operation we just described:

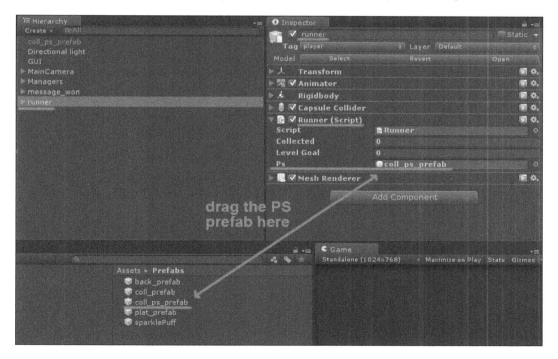

How it works...

Using the particle system, we solved our problem of playing an audio clip on a game object that is about to be destroyed. Instead of putting the audio clip in the collectible item, we put it in a particle system prefab that we instantiate in the scene whenever a collectible is gathered by the player.

At the same time, we provide clear, consistent feedback to the player that they achieve something good when the character hits a collectible.

Game options – volume level

Among the extra features we are adding to the prototype, we'd like to provide an example of options screen functionality by showing you how to set up a horizontal slider to control the volume of the background music carpet.

Getting ready

For this recipe, we will use the **bkgd_01** audio clip we imported at the beginning of this chapter. Open your project in Unity and ensure that **bkgd_01** is configured in the **Inspector** window, as we did in the first recipe of this chapter.

How to do it...

1. To make **Option Screen** for the prototype, we begin by creating a new scene and naming it **Option Screen**.
2. Next, add an empty game object to the scene and name it **GUI**.
3. Add an **Audio Source** component to the **GUI** game object in the scene. Remember that whenever you want a game object to play a sound, an Audio Source component must be attached to it.
4. Now we add a script to the game object, with the instructions to draw the interface and control its functionality. Create a new C# script and name it **VolumeController**.
5. Double-click on the script to open it in **Monodevelop**.
6. First of all, we need two public variables, one to store the reference to the audio clip we want to be played, and the other to store the actual volume level based on the position of the horizontal slider. We make this second variable static so that we can access its value anywhere. Add the following lines to the script:

```
public AudioClip bkgdClip;
static private float volumeLevel;
```

7. Now we need the `OnGUI()` function to draw the slider on screen and set the volume level. Add these lines to the script:

```
void OnGUI(){
    volumeLevel = GUI.HorizontalSlider( new Rect(30,30,110, 30),
volumeLevel, 0.0f,                    10.0f);
}
```

8. To end with scripting, we need to add a line to the `Update()` function to check whether the volume at which the sound is played is the same as the volume that is set on the slider. This is done with the following instruction in the `Update()` function:

```
void Update () {

    audio.volume = volumeLevel;

}
```

9. The final step is to drag the audio clip asset named `bkgd_01` from the **Project** panel into the **Audio Clip** slot of the script, as shown in the following screenshot:

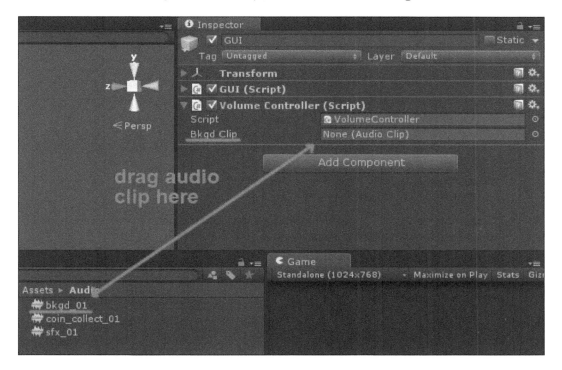

How it works...

The horizontal slider works as expected. By moving the cursor left or right you adjust the volume the background music is played at, in a range that goes from volume = 0 to volume = 10.

Let's improve the **Options Screen** functionality by allowing the user to toggle the audio clip on or off with the next recipe.

Game options – toggling audio

In this recipe, we will show you how toggle buttons for the user interface of games made with Unity can be created and managed.

Getting ready

Like the previous recipe, you must have the **Options Screen** scene loaded in the Editor and the **GUI** script open in **Monodevelop**.

How to do it...

1. Let's begin by creating a `bool` variable to control whether the toggle is on or off. We do this by adding the following declaration at the top of the script:

   ```
   private bool toggleAudio = true;
   ```

2. Next, we create the **toggle** button on the screen by adding the following line inside the `OnGUI()` function:

   ```
   toggleAudio = GUI.Toggle(new Rect(100, 30, 10, 10),
      toggleAudio, "Toggle Audio");
   ```

3. Now, in the `Update()` function, we add a line to ensure that the audio is enabled, depending on the `toggleAudio` value:

   ```
   audio.enabled = toggleAudio;
   ```

4. The following screenshot provides the complete `GUI` script we used for the **Options Screen** scene:

```
1  using UnityEngine;
2  using System.Collections;
3
4  public class VolumeController : MonoBehaviour {
5
6      public AudioClip bkgdClip;
7      static public float volumeLevel;
8
9      private bool toggleAudio = true;
10
11     // Use this for initialization
12     void Start () {
13
14     }
15
16     // Update is called once per frame
17     void Update () {
18
19         audio.volume = volumeLevel;
20
21         audio.enabled = toggleAudio;
22
23     }
24
25     void OnGUI(){
26
27         volumeLevel = GUI.HorizontalSlider( new Rect(30,30,110, 30), volumeLevel, 0.0f, 10.0f);
28
29         toggleAudio = GUI.Toggle(new Rect(10, 10, 100, 30), toggleAudio, "Toggle Audio");
30
31     }
32 }
```

Playing videoclips in the scene

In the last recipe of this chapter, we'll learn how a video can be displayed in the game scene. It is a useful feature—very handy for computer graphics scenes or cut scenes or if you want to include a monitor displaying a video clip in your game scene.

Getting ready

You need two things for this recipe. Firstly, install QuickTime on your PC, if you don't have it already. Without QuickTime, Unity cannot import video clips properly. The QuickTime installer can be downloaded from http://www.apple.com/quicktime/download/.

Next, we need a video clip. If you don't have a clip to use, you can load the video clip we have provided with the content of this book.

How to do it...

1. Exit and launch Unity again, after QuickTime is installed.

2. Create a new folder in your project and name it `Videos`.

3. Access the folder and right-click to import a new asset, as we did many times.

4. Unity imports all major video file formats. In this case, we opted for an MPEG file. Select the file named **video_01** (or any other video you want to use) and import it into the project.

5. Leave the settings in the **Inspector** window alone for now. We don't need to edit them.

6. Next, we need a game object to project the video on. Let's use **Quad** for this. Quads are single-faced, rectangular surfaces that are instantiated in the game scene like any other polygon available in the **GameObject** menu of Unity (cubes, spheres, and cylinders). Quads are made of just two triangles/faces, so they are very light game objects that provide a flat surface that proves useful when we need to display flat textures, plain text, or video clips in the game scene.

7. Create **Quad** in the scene by navigating to **GameObject | Create Other | Quad**, as shown in the following screenshot:

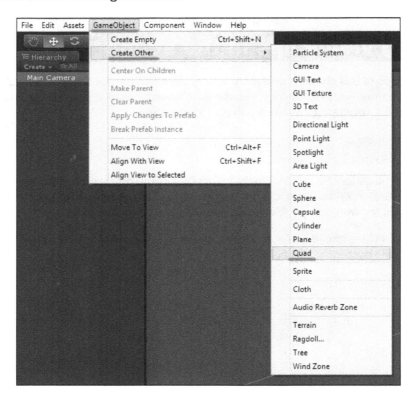

8. Name the **Quad** screen, place it in front of the camera, and size it as you please. Take into consideration the fact that the video we have provided is designed to be displayed in HD resolution.

9. Now drag the movie clip from the **Project** panel onto **Quad** in the scene, as you would do with a material, as shown in this screenshot:

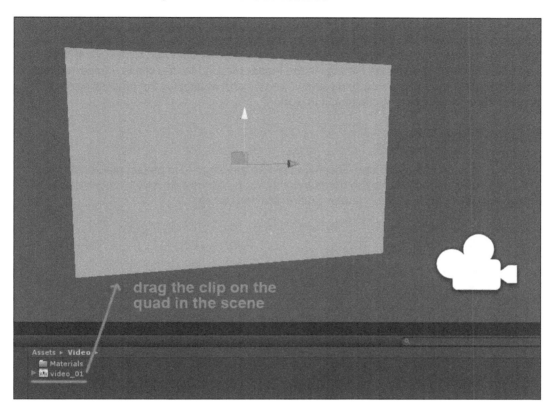

10. Create a new C# script and name it **VideoPlayer**.

11. Open the script in **Monodevelop**.

12. Assuming we are fine with playing the video as the scene begins, we can play it by adding the following lines to the Start () function of the script:

```
void Start () {

    MovieTexture mt =
      (MovieTexture)renderer.material.mainTexture;
    mt.Play();

}
```

13. To complete the task, drag the script onto the **Quad** in the scene (named **Screen**).

How it works...

Video clips are added to game objects in the scene as you would do with any other material. The difference is that, with video clips, the material is obtained from a video clip, instead of a texture.

That said, a very important aspect when dealing with videos is to correctly code them. On one side, you need quality, and on the other side, you need to keep the file as small as possible. Take into consideration the fact that importing long videos in Unity can take several minutes, and that whenever you change settings in the **Inspector** window, the clip is reimported and processed. This means you may find yourself waiting and waiting for the processing to be done, before being able to getting back to work!

There's more...

With Unity, it is pretty easy to add videos and create the controls to pause, play, or stop the video. We recommend referring to the manual at `http://docs.unity3d.com/Manual/class-MovieTexture.html` to delve more into this matter.

8
Sprites, Spritesheets, and 2D Animation in Unity

In this chapter, we'll cover the following recipes:

- ▶ Setting up sprites
- ▶ Multiple sprites
- ▶ Animating with spritesheets
- ▶ Preparing character sprites
- ▶ Parenting sprites
- ▶ Keyframe sprite animation

Introduction

Though Unity is basically a three-dimensional engine, it provides several excellent tools to create full two-dimensional games as well. As most indie games are 2D, we think you can take advantage of learning at least the basics of managing sprites in Unity. With this chapter, we aim to make you proficient with sprites, spritesheets, and 2D animation techniques.

Sprites can be defined as 2D images that get animated in a larger scene. Think of any classic 2D platform video game, such as Nintendo's *Super Mario Bros*. There is a background image (usually static), and there is a character running and jumping across the screen. That character is a sprite.

A sprite is created by importing a texture in the project and setting it as a **Sprite** type.

Setting up sprites

In this recipe, we explore the operations required to set up a 2D image as a **Sprite** type in Unity.

Getting ready

You can start an entirely new project for this chapter, or open the project we are already working on. In either case, add a new folder to the **Assets** directory of the project and name it **Sprites**. As we already did this operation in the previous chapters, we won't repeat the steps here.

How to do it...

1. Import the **2D_Sprites** package we have provided with the contents of this book to your project. If you don't remember how to do it, right-click on the **Sprites** folder you just created and select **Import Package/Custom Package...** from the menu, as shown in this screenshot:

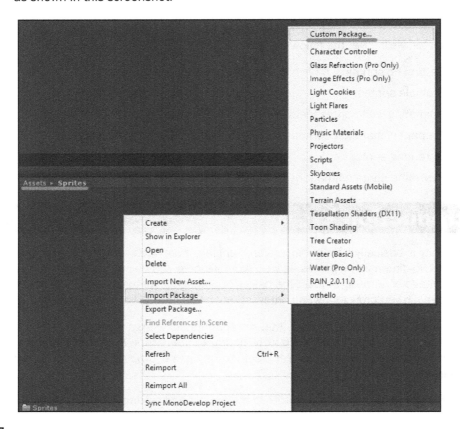

2. The package contains two images named **2D_pose** and **2D_walk**. Ensure that both are selected in the **Import** panel and then hit **Import**, as shown in the following screenshot:

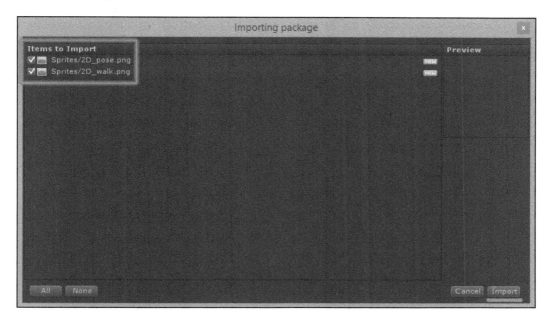

3. Once the importing process is complete, access the **Sprites** folder and select the first picture, **2D_pose**.

4. Go to the **Inspector** window and set the **Texture Type** property to **Sprite**.

5. A **Sprite Mode** property should appear, right below **Texture Type**. Select **Single** from the drop-down menu.

The **Pixel to Units** property defines how many pixels in the sprite are there in one unit (1 unit is 1 meter in Unity) in the game world. We don't need to edit this property; you can leave it at its default value of **100**. Remember, however, that this gets important if you plan to use physics in your game. We recommend the guide at `http://answers.unity3d.com/questions/736142/what-is-good-practice-to-set-pixels-to-units-to-an.html` for this matter. Click on **Apply** to save these settings. You can refer to the following screenshot to understand the last steps:

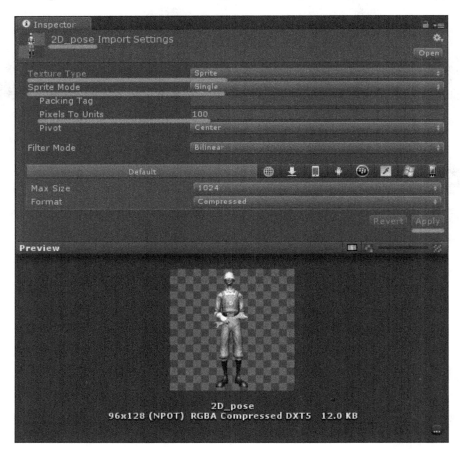

6. The base sprite for our 2D character is ready. Create new **Empty GameObject** in **Scene** and name it **2DCharacter**, as shown in this screenshot:

7. Now you can drag the sprite named **2D_pose** onto **2DCharacter** in the scene. Once you do so, a **Sprite Renderer** component is automatically attached to **2DCharacter**, and a **Default-Sprite** material is created, with the **2D_pose** sprite as the **Material** entry of the component, as shown in the following screenshot:

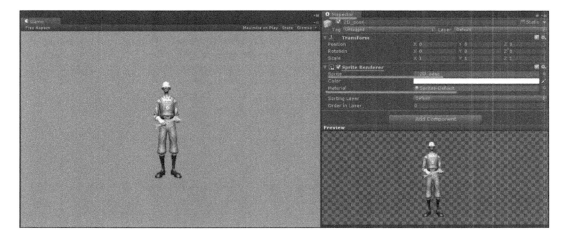

How it works...

A sprite is a 2D image applied to a flat object on a screen. We set our sprite as **Single Mode** in the **Inspector** window, as this sprite contains only one image, representing the static pose of our 2D character. Then we applied the sprite through a material to an empty game object on screen, as we already did with 3D assets.

There's more...

The **Sprite Renderer** component, which Unity automatically applied to the game object we dragged the image on, is a default component of Unity, and its task is to display images on the screen. It requires a sprite texture to render and refers to a default sprite material that can be instantiated at will in the game scene, displaying different textures for different game objects. This way you don't have to worry about creating several materials when you have many sprites on screen. They will all use the same material with different textures!

The Sprite Renderer also allows us to define the depth order in which sprites must be rendered on the screen. Though 2D games don't operate in the third dimension (z), it may still come in handy to put different sprites in a specific order if the flat images overlap at some points and you want one specific chunk of the sprite to be rendered above the others. We will discuss these features in the following recipes, but those of you who want to delve more into the **Sprite Renderer** component right now can check out the manual at `http://docs. unity3d.com/Manual/class-SpriteRenderer.html`.

Multiple sprites

Though sprites can consist of a single image, they generally require many. In traditional sprite animation, animation clips are obtained by displaying several images in a sequence, each representing a stage (or keyframe) of the complete animation. These groups of images in sequence are referred to as spritesheets and they are the building blocks of sprite animation.

In the following recipe, we show you how to set a Multiple Mode Sprite Texture to create a cycle that shows our 2D sprite walking.

Getting ready

You should have already imported both the sprites we provided during the previous lesson, so do it now if you haven't.

How to do it...

1. Move to the **Project** panel and access the **Sprites** folder. Now select **2D_walk** to access the image properties in the **Inspector** window.

2. Set **Texture Type** to **Sprite** as we did before, but this time, set **Sprite Mode** to **Multiple**, as this sprite contains several steps of the walking cycle. You can refer to the following screenshot:

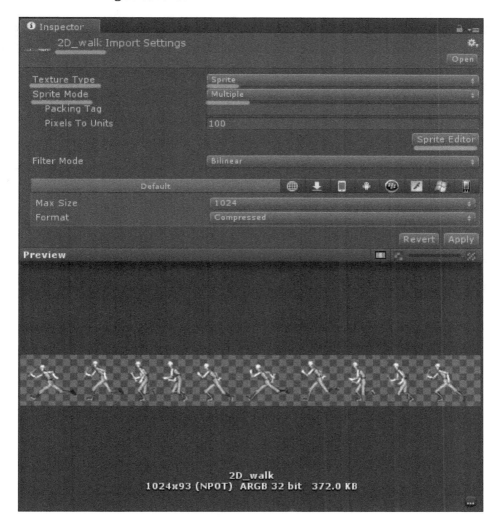

3. To open the **Sprite Editor** panel, click on the **Sprite Editor** button that just appeared.

4. Here, we can make arrangements so that Unity splits the image the way we need it to work for the animation cycle. Right now, the image is displayed as whole containing many instances of Mario. What we want is that each instance in the image gets nicely separated from the others by a selection box. To do this, hit the **Slice** button in the top-left corner of the panel, as shown in this screenshot:

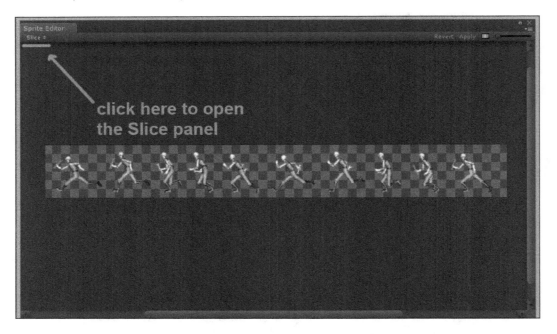

5. Set the **Type** property to **Automatic**, the **Pivot** property to **Center**, and the **Method** property to **Delete Existing**.

6. Don't bother about the **Minimum Size** property, for now. Instead, hit **Slice** to apply the slicing process. As a result, each Mario instance in the image should now be surrounded by a thin white line, as shown in the following screenshot:

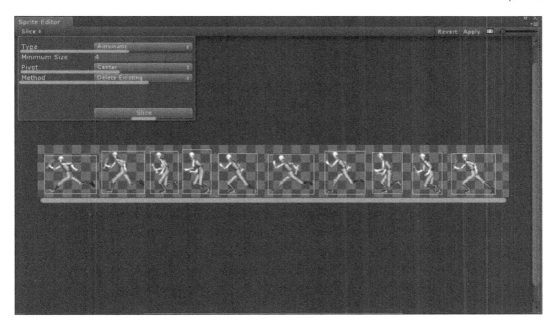

7. Now hit **Apply** in the top-right corner of the panel to apply the edits to our multiple sprites, as shown in this screenshot:

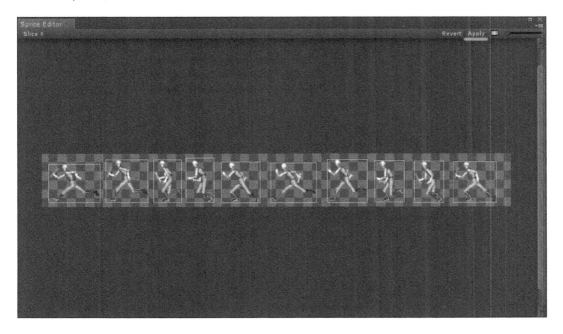

8. The sprite has been now split into 17 chunks, each representing a step, or frame, of the cycle of the animation of walking. You can verify this by expanding the hierarchy of **2D_walk** in the **Project** panel, as shown here:

How it works...

As we discussed in a previous chapter, combining several small images into a larger image is an efficient technique to save memory when making video games. It also allows us to have several sprites on the same image rendered with a single draw call (a technique usually referred to as batching). See `http://gamedev.stackexchange.com/questions/32910/what-is-the-technical-definition-of-sprite-batching` for more information.

Sprites can be animated by putting several frames, each representing a stage of the complete animation, in sequence on a single image, which is called spritesheet or texture atlas. After importing such an image, it can be set in the **Inspector** window as a multiple sprite, and then we can use that sequence to animate the sprite. This is the topic of our next recipe.

There's more...

If the automatic slicing process doesn't work perfectly when splitting a multiple sprite, it is possible to slice a multiple sprite based on based on a grid defined by the user. This technique works fine when all frames in the multiple sprite are of the same width and height, which was not our case with the walking animation for Mario. To know more about the **Sprite Editor** features, refer to `http://docs.unity3d.com/Manual/SpriteEditor.html`. In the following recipe, we will show you how to perform this task.

Animating with spritesheets

Now that the spritesheet with the animation cycle is correctly split up, we can use the multiple sprites to create a walking animation for our character.

In this recipe, we will use the spritesheet we set up in the previous recipe to create an animation cycle for a character sprite.

Getting ready

We keep up from where we left, so have Unity open and be ready to follow our leads!

How to do it...

1. Let's start with a clean game scene. Remove all game objects from the scene, except for **Main Camera**.

2. Create a new game object in the scene and name it **2D_Walker**.

3. Drag the **2D_walk** sprite from the **Project** panel onto **2D_Walker** in the scene, as shown in the following screenshot:

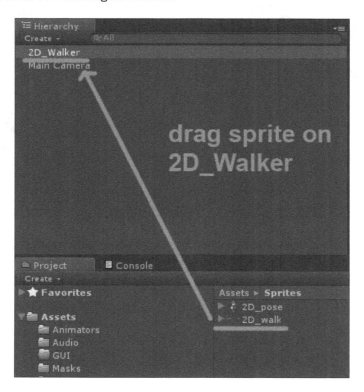

4. The **Sprite Renderer** component has now been added to **2D_Walker**. In the **Sprite** property, you should have a frame named **2D_walk_0**. If you don't, you can click on the small button in the bottom-right corner of the **Sprite Renderer** panel in the **Inspector** window, and select the frame named **2D_walk_0** from the window that opens, as shown in this screenshot:

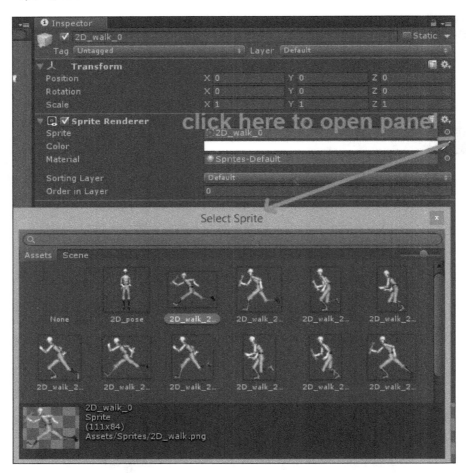

5. The next step is to add an animation clip to the object to store the frames of the walking cycle. From top main menu of Unity, navigate to **Window | Animation** to open the **Animation** panel, as shown in the following screenshot:

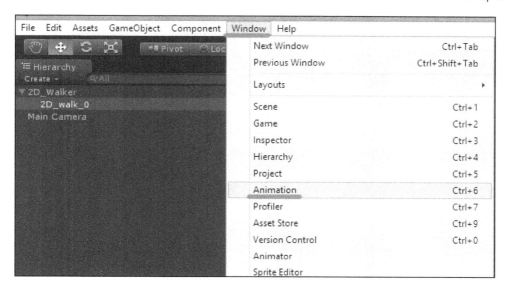

6. Click on the small arrows in the left-top corner of the panel to add a new clip, as shown here:

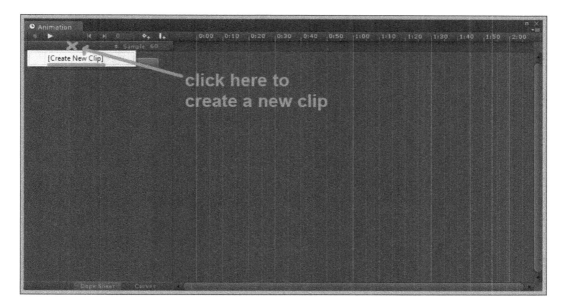

7. A window opens, where we need to set a destination folder to save the animation clip. Name the clip `walk` and save it in the **Anims** folder inside **Assets**, which is in **Sprites**, as shown in the following screenshot:

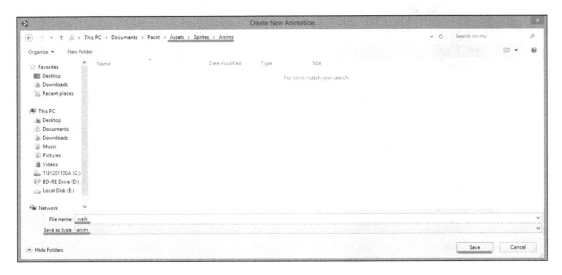

8. Now expand the hierarchy of **2D_walk** in the **Project** panel to display all its frames, and select them by pressing *Shift* and clicking, as shown in the following screenshot:

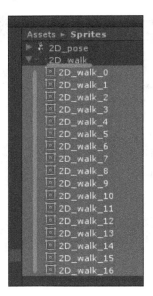

9. Drag all the frames onto the **Animation** panel, as shown here:

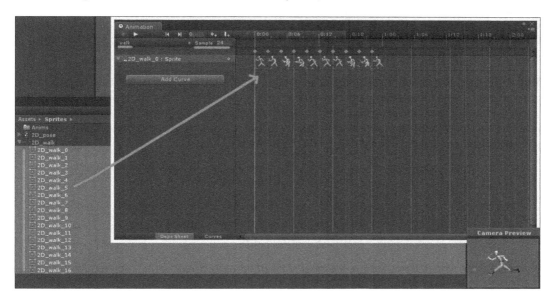

10. Check whether the **Sample** parameter is set to 24 frames (instead of the default value of 60, because 60 frames per second would be too much for this walking cycle), as displayed in the previous screenshot.

11. Click on the small red recording button in the **Animation** panel so that the clip gets saved. When you hit the play button to launch the game in Unity, you should see Mario walking in a looped cycle.

How it works...

Once a spritesheet is split into several frames, Unity is automatically capable of displaying them within an animation clip in a given order and at a given frame rate. The clip is then attached to the **Animation** component of a game object so that the game object can perform the animation clip defined in the spritesheet.

There's more...

Using spritesheets is not the only way to animate sprites. Actually, there are cases where keyframe animation may be preferred.

With keyframe animation, a clip is obtained as a sequence of keyframes on a timeline. In each keyframe, the character is set in a pose that is a step of the final animation we aim to create. Unity takes care of interpolating the movement of each individual animated part of the sprite between one keyframe and the next. Thus, when we play the animation clip on the timeline, the result we get is coherent, progressive animation.

This is the same concept of spritesheet animation after all; the difference is that no predrawn spritesheet is required with skeletal animation and the character can be directly animated. As such, animating sprites with keyframe animation is actually an optimization technique, as it reduces the amount of data required to store several spritesheets in the project. We suggest you visit the following links to go deeper into this matter:

 ▶ http://www.reddit.com/r/gamedev/comments/27ede3/sprite_
   animation_vs_skeletal_animation/

 ▶ http://www.ganggarrison.com/forums/index.php?topic=27445.0

 ▶ http://www.gamasutra.com/view/news/176663/5_tips_for_making_
   great_animations_for_2D_games.php

In order to use skeletal animation, the character must be provided with so-called joints. This is the topic of our next recipe.

Preparing the character sprites

In this recipe, we will see how the individual sprites belonging to a character are prepared for keyframe animation.

Getting ready

We are going to create an entirely new character for this recipe, so start by creating a new scene in your Unity project.

Next, import the **keyframe_anim** PNG image we have provided with the contents of this book to the **Sprites** folder located in **Assets**. We've done this many times so far. The image contains the blocks to actually build up two characters, an orc and a knight. We will use the knight for this recipe, and once you have learned the process, you can make the orc or even mix the two characters to get something original!

How to do it...

1. Select the PNG image you just imported. Then set **Texture Type** to **Sprite** and **Sprite Mode** to **Multiple** in the **Inspector** window, as shown in the following screenshot:

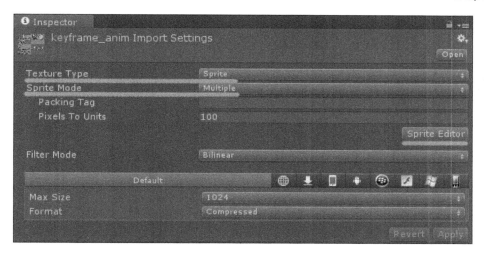

2. Click on the **Sprite Editor** button to open **Sprite Editor**.

3. Use the **Slice** menu, which is set to **Automatic**, to slice the image into its individual chunks, as we did before. If the automatic slicing method fails, you can edit the image manually by dragging the corners of each chunk. Refer to the following screenshot, showing a failed slice that we are going to fix manually:

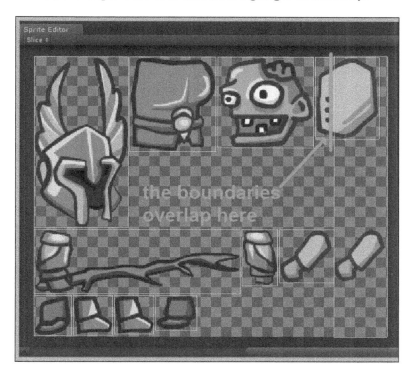

4. To fix **Slice**, select **Sprite** by clicking on it to display its slicing boundaries. Then drag one of its corners to resize the boundaries themselves, as shown in the following screenshot:

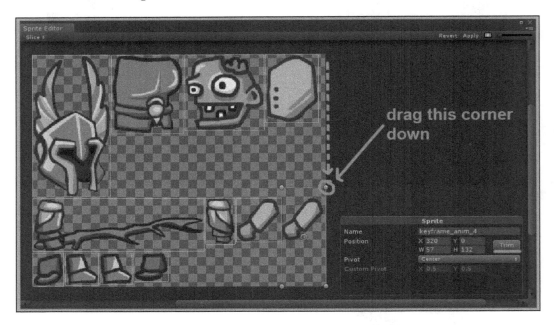

5. When the sprite is selected, a small panel opens in the corner of the window. Hit the **Trim** button to have Unity finalize the resized boundary.

6. In the same panel, it is possible to enter a name for each individual sprite chunk. Once you are done resizing the slicing boundaries, name each part of the knight we are going to use as follows: **Head**, **Body**, **Arm_L**, **Arm_R**, **Foot_L**, and **Foot_R**. Remember that the right arm is the arm with the stick. You shouldn't have problems assigning the other names.

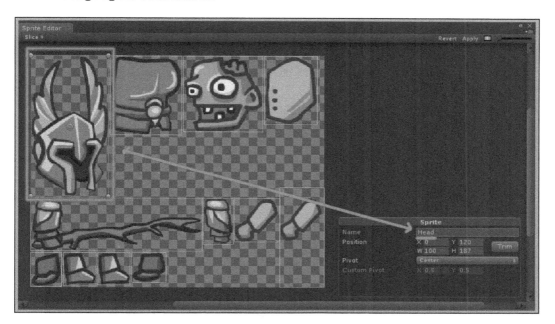

7. Another operation required is to correctly set the so-called pivot point of each sprite. The pivot point is the spot on the sprites that acts as reference point for any translation and rotation of the sprite. Depending on each individual part, it may be necessary to move the pivot point from the center to another position; for example, the pivot point of the head goes where the neck is supposed to be, the arm's pivot goes on the shoulder, and so on. This screenshot should help you understand what we mean:

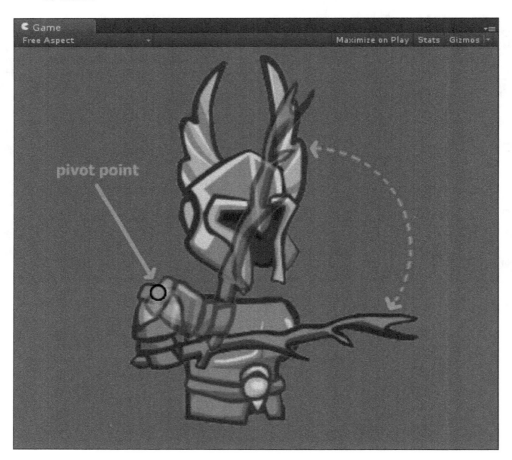

To move the pivot, simply select it and drag it where you want. The following screenshot shows what we did:

8. Hit **Apply** in the top-right corner when you are done with editing the sprites. If you expand the hierarchy of **keyframe_anim** in the **Project** panel, you should see the parts we named, as shown in this screenshot:

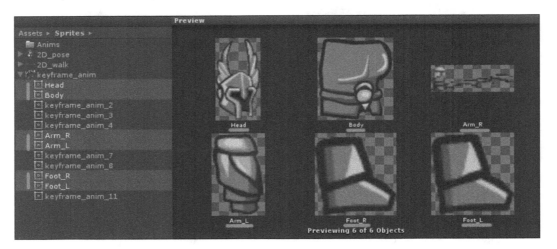

How it works...

In this recipe, we saw how to slice a spritesheet with the **Sprite Editor**. We also saw the operations required to resize the slicing boundaries, place the pivot points on the sprites, and name the individual chunks.

In the next recipe, we will learn how to parent these chunks to actually animate an assembled character.

Parenting sprites

Inverse kinematics is a technique consisting of placing joints between elements that move together so that the movement of one element influences the other elements it is attached to. Our body, for example, is a collection of parts connected with joints that move according to rules of inverse kinematics. When we raise an arm, the arm, forearm and the hand, as well as the individual fingers, all follow according to their joints.

By setting the pivot points on the sprite chunks at the end of the previous recipe, we actually defined the joints to build the inverse kinematics for the character. Now we will parent the pieces together by their pivot points so that we can finally animate the character.

Getting ready

We keep up from where we left, so have your project open and be ready to follow our instructions.

How to do it...

1. Let's start by creating new **Empty GameObject** in the scene and naming it `Character`.

2. Select all pieces of the knight (six in total) and drag them onto **Character** in the scene.

3. Unity opens a window asking us to save the animation clip we are about to create. Go to **Assets | Sprites | Anims** and name the clip `attack`, as shown in the following screenshot:

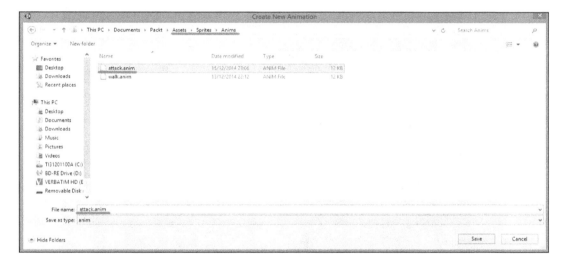

4. Uncheck **Root Motion** and check **Animate Physics** in the **Animator** panel in the **Inspector** window, (just as we did before) as shown in this screenshot (if you don't remember what root motion is, you can check it out in *Chapter 1, Importing 3D Models and Animations*):

5. Now we can actually parent the pieces belonging to the knight. All the chunks should be in the scene by now. If they are not, drag them one at a time into the scene.

6. Let's start by parenting **Body** to **Character**. Select **Body** in the **Hierarchy** window and drag it onto **Character**.

7. **Body** will be our reference for all other pieces. Now drag **Head** onto **Body**.

8. Then drag **Arm_L** and **Arm_R** onto **body**.

9. Finally, drag **Foot_L** and **Foot_R** similarly. The following screenshot shows **Hierarchy** you should see in your own editor:

10. If you check out your character in the editor scene or the game scene, you may notice that the body parts of the knight actually overlap and produce a few perspective glitches. As we learned in the recipe titled *Setting Up Sprites* of this chapter, when a sprite is instantiated in the game scene, Unity automatically provides it with a **Sprite Renderer** component. By inspecting the **Sprite Render** panel in the **Inspector** window, you should see two properties we didn't mention so far: **Sorting Layer** and **Order in Layer**.

11. **Sorting Layer** defines the order in which the sprites are rendered on screen on a macro scale, so to say. You can use layers to send all background elements of a scene to the back so that animated sprites can be drawn above them. To create a new sorting layer, click on the drop-down menu in the panel (which should be on default right now) and select **Add Sorting Layer...**, as shown in the following screenshot:

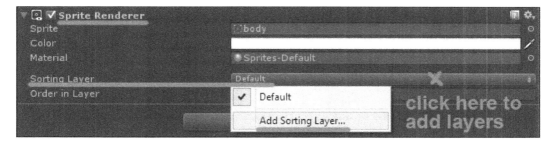

12. **Order in Layer** defines the order inside a layer created by the user: the higher the number, the closer the sprite to the eyes of the player.

13. In our case, we could assign indexes as follows: 0 to **Body**, 1 to **Head** and **Foot_R**, 2 to **Arm_R**, and -1 to **Arm_L** and **Foot_L**. Here is a screenshot that shows the result we should get:

How it works...

Parenting game objects in Unity is really easy; all it takes is to drag one object onto another in the **Hierarchy** panel. Once two or more objects are parented together, you can move, rotate, or scale the entire group by manipulating the highest element in the hierarchy, but you can also manipulate the individual child objects by selecting them. The **Sprite Renderer** component also allows you to set single sprites from the same image in the correct rendering order by defining positive or negative indexes.

With the pivot points set and the parts correctly parented together, we are ready to finally animate the knight, which we will cover in our next recipe.

Keyframe sprite animation

Now, let's learn how to create a simple **attack** animation clip for our sprite character using keyframes instead of a spritesheet.

Keyframe animation is a complex topic, and we cannot fully address it in a single recipe. Nevertheless, we'll use this opportunity to cover the basic principles so that you can get a grasp of the procedure.

Getting ready

Again, we keep up from where we left. Have your project open and be ready to follow our instructions.

How to do it...

1. Open the **Animation** panel by going to **Window | Animation**, as shown in the following screenshot:

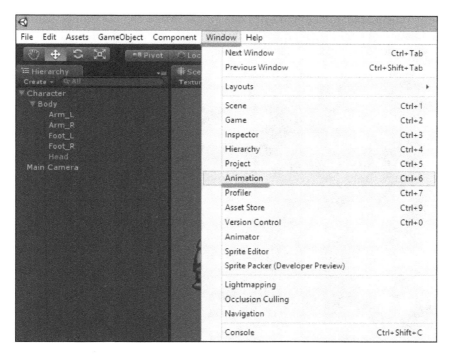

2. Select **Character** in **Scene**. Then click on the drop-down menu in the **Animation** panel to set **attack** as the active clip, as shown in this screenshot:

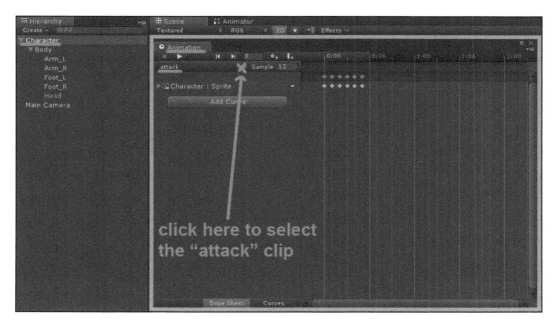

3. Set a reasonable number of keyframes for the attack clip; 24 frames per seconds is a good starting point. Then hit the recording button to start recording the clip. You can refer to the following screenshot to ensure that you are doing it right:

4. With the record button pressed, move the timeline cursor to half the clip, that is, at 12 seconds, as shown in the following screenshot:

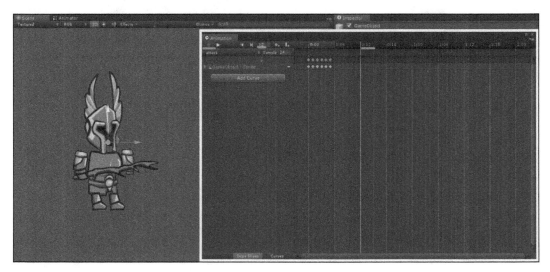

5. Go to the **Scene**, select **Arm_R** (in **Scene** or from the **Hierarchy** window) and move the cursor close to the corner of the boundary (the blue dots). The cursor should change to a rotating icon. Grab the corner and rotate the arm around the pivot we set earlier. Here is a screenshot that shows the result you should get:

6. By doing so, we created two keyframes for **Arm_R**: one frame in the position it was at 0 seconds of the clip, and another frame at 12 seconds, with the rotation we applied. To close this attacking loop, we need to set the final position keyframe, which is at the same position we started with.

Set the time line at frame 24 (by setting the value as we did before). Then click on the small button with a rhombus and a **+** icon to add a keyframe at second 24. Please refer to the following screenshot:

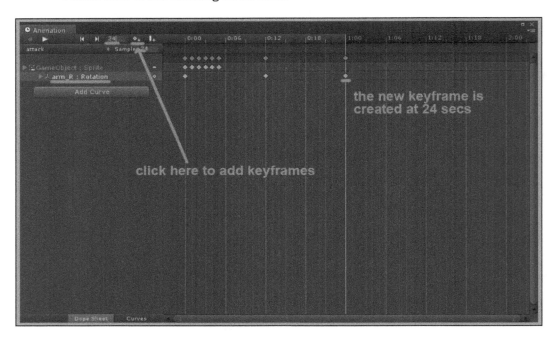

7. Now, with **Arm_R** still selected in the scene, move to the **Animation** panel and select the frame at **0:00**. Then go to the **Transform** component panel in the **Inspector** window and copy (right-click and select **Copy**) the **Rotation** value on the z axis, as shown in this screenshot:

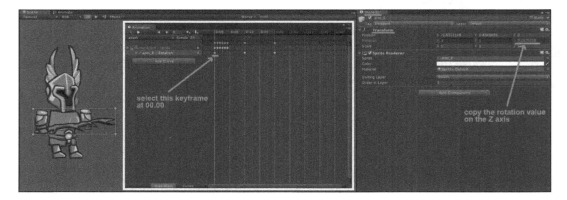

8. The last step is to paste the **Rotation** value at **0:00** on the frame at **24:00**. Select the frame and then paste (right-click and select **Paste**) the rotation value on the *z* axis. If you did this right, the arm should get back to its starting position. Please refer to the following screenshot:

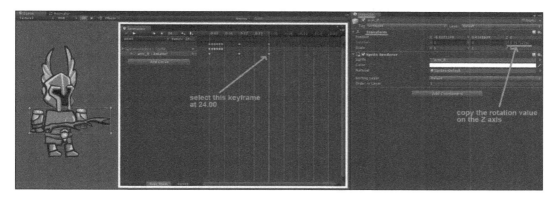

9. You can now test the result. Disable the record button and then try hitting play on the **Animation** panel. Hopefully, the knight will start swinging the stick it holds in its right-hand!

How it works...

With respect to its general principles, keyframe animation is easy to understand, as it consists of setting keyframes and then moving single body parts in the position we want at that keyframe. Unity takes care of making the transitions between frames so that at the end of the animation process, we perceive a meaningful sequence instead of a collection of static frames.

The hard part comes with tweaking the animations to make them part of the characterization, which goes beyond the scope of this book.

The interface of the **Animation** panel may not look friendly at a first glance, so we recommend repeating this last group of recipes and creating an animated orc with the other sprites available in the sprite atlas we have provided.

There's more...

We have just scratched the surface of animation and keyframe animation here, as several other options and tools are available; for example, transitions between frames can be adjusted using curves to slow movements down (or speed them up), and make animations nicer and more believable. Animation curves have recently gone legacy (so they are still supported but not recommended anymore), but the manual at `http://docs.unity3d.com/Manual/animeditor-AnimationCurves.html` still provides all the explanations you will require to make the most out of them.

For those of you who are interested in animation in general, we recommend the following links to begin with:

▶ `http://en.wikipedia.org/wiki/Key_frame`
▶ `http://graphics.cs.cmu.edu/nsp/course/15-464/Spring11/lectures/lec02.pdf`

Dudes, animation is massive topic!

There is also this link that I love, at `http://the12principles.tumblr.com/`.

Last, but absolutely not least, is the king of animation manuals: The *Animator's Survival Kit* by former Disney's Richard Williams. It is available at popular online stores.

Index

H

Heads-Up Display (HUD) 166

I

image file formats
  URL, for wiki 41
imported animations
  configuring, in Unity Inspector 32-36
imported FBX file
  configuring, into Unity 26-29
Inspector panel 4
Instantiate() function 125
interface
  about 2
  Editor window 4
  Game scene 4
  Hierarchy panel 3
  Inspector panel 4
  Main Menu 3
  Project panel 4
inverse kinematics 224

K

keyframe animation 217
keyframe sprite animation
  used, for creating simple attack
    animation clip 228-233

L

layers 90
level design 123

M

masks
  creating 90-93
materials
  about 40, 48
  animating 63-65
  creating 48-53
  names, setting in Maya 53-55
  URL, for articles 40
  URL, for manual 104

Maya
  about 16
  FBX file, exporting from 22-25
  names, setting of materials 53-55
  references 16
  scene, setting up in 16-20
  URL, for user guide 32
Maya Embedded Language. *See* **MEL**
Maya LT 20
Mean 2
Mecanim 37, 67, 68, 97
MEL
  about 31
  URL, for list of exporting commands 31
MEL script
  URL, for example 31
Movie Texture
  URL 202
Multiple Mode Sprite Texture
  setting 208-212

N

new scene
  loading, at runtime 163-166
normal maps
  URL, for Wikipedia links 100
number, of collected items
  displaying 172-176

O

object pooling 137
OnCollisionEnter() function
  URL, for description 121
OnCollisionEnter() function,
    versus OnTriggerEnter()
  reference link 153
OnGUI() method
  used, for displaying game data 169-172

P

packages
  importing 105-107
particles 187

Thank you for buying
Unity 2D Game Development Cookbook

About Packt Publishing

Packt, pronounced 'packed', published its first book, *Mastering phpMyAdmin for Effective MySQL Management*, in April 2004, and subsequently continued to specialize in publishing highly focused books on specific technologies and solutions.

Our books and publications share the experiences of your fellow IT professionals in adapting and customizing today's systems, applications, and frameworks. Our solution-based books give you the knowledge and power to customize the software and technologies you're using to get the job done. Packt books are more specific and less general than the IT books you have seen in the past. Our unique business model allows us to bring you more focused information, giving you more of what you need to know, and less of what you don't.

Packt is a modern yet unique publishing company that focuses on producing quality, cutting-edge books for communities of developers, administrators, and newbies alike. For more information, please visit our website at www.packtpub.com.

Writing for Packt

We welcome all inquiries from people who are interested in authoring. Book proposals should be sent to author@packtpub.com. If your book idea is still at an early stage and you would like to discuss it first before writing a formal book proposal, then please contact us; one of our commissioning editors will get in touch with you.

We're not just looking for published authors; if you have strong technical skills but no writing experience, our experienced editors can help you develop a writing career, or simply get some additional reward for your expertise.

Unity 3D UI Essentials

ISBN: 978-1-78355-361-7   Paperback: 280 pages

Leverage the power of the new and improved UI system for Unity to enhance your games and apps

1. Discover how to build efficient UI layouts coping with multiple resolutions and screen sizes.

2. In-depth overview of all the new UI features that give you creative freedom to drive your game development to new heights.

3. Walk through many different examples of UI layout from simple 2D overlays to in-game 3D implementations.

Unity Game Development Scripting

ISBN: 978-1-78355-363-1   Paperback: 202 pages

Write efficient C# scripts to create modular key game elements that are usable for any kind of Unity project

1. Write customizable scripts that are easy to adjust to suit the needs of different projects.

2. Combine your knowledge of modular scripting elements to build a complete game.

3. Build key game features, from player inventories to friendly and enemy artificial intelligence.

Please check **www.PacktPub.com** for information on our titles

Unity Game Development Blueprints

ISBN: 978-1-78355-365-5   Paperback: 318 pages

Explore the various enticing features of Unity and learn how to develop awesome games

1. Create a wide variety of projects with Unity in multiple genres and formats.

2. Complete art assets with clear step-by-step examples and instructions to complete all tasks using Unity, C#, and MonoDevelop.

3. Develop advanced internal and external environments for games in 2D and 3D.

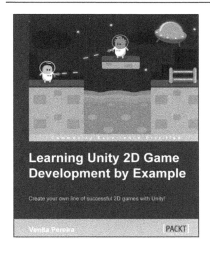

Learning Unity 2D Game Development by Example

ISBN: 978-1-78355-904-6   Paperback: 266 pages

Create your own line of successful 2D games with Unity!

1. Dive into 2D game development with no previous experience.

2. Learn how to use the new Unity 2D toolset.

3. Create and deploy your very own 2D game with confidence.

Please check **www.PacktPub.com** for information on our titles

www.ingramcontent.com/pod-product-compliance
Lightning Source LLC
Chambersburg PA
CBHW060539060326
40690CB00017B/3542